OECD CENTRE FOR CO-OPERATION WITH NON-MEMBERS

Reviews of National Policies for Education

Latvia

OECD

ORGANISATION FOR ECONOMIC CO-OPERATION AND DEVELOPMENT

ORGANISATION FOR ECONOMIC CO-OPERATION AND DEVELOPMENT

Pursuant to Article 1 of the Convention signed in Paris on 14th December 1960, and which came into force on 30th September 1961, the Organisation for Economic Co-operation and Development (OECD) shall promote policies designed:

- to achieve the highest sustainable economic growth and employment and a rising standard of living in Member countries, while maintaining financial stability, and thus to contribute to the development of the world economy;
- to contribute to sound economic expansion in Member as well as non-member countries in the process of economic development; and
- to contribute to the expansion of world trade on a multilateral, non-discriminatory basis in accordance with international obligations.

The original Member countries of the OECD are Austria, Belgium, Canada, Denmark, France, Germany, Greece, Iceland, Ireland, Italy, Luxembourg, the Netherlands, Norway, Portugal, Spain, Sweden, Switzerland, Turkey, the United Kingdom and the United States. The following countries became Members subsequently through accession at the dates indicated hereafter: Japan (28th April 1964), Finland (28th January 1969), Australia (7th June 1971), New Zealand (29th May 1973), Mexico (18th May 1994), the Czech Republic (21st December 1995), Hungary (7th May 1996), Poland (22nd November 1996), Korea (12th December 1996) and the Slovak Republic (14h December 2000). The Commission of the European Communities takes part in the work of the OECD (Article 13 of the OECD Convention).

OECD CENTRE FOR CO-OPERATION WITH NON-MEMBERS

The OECD Centre for Co-operation with Non-Members (CCNM) promotes and co-ordinates OECD's policy dialogue and co-operation with economies outside the OECD area. The OECD currently maintains policy co-operation with approximately 70 non-Member economies.

The essence of CCNM co-operative programmes with non-Members is to make the rich and varied assets of the OECD available beyond its current Membership to interested non-Members. For example, the OECD's unique co-operative working methods that have been developed over many years; a stock of best practices across all areas of public policy experiences among Members; on-going policy dialogue among senior representatives from capitals, reinforced by reciprocal peer pressure; and the capacity to address interdisciplinary issues. All of this is supported by a rich historical database and strong analytical capacity within the Secretariat. Likewise, Member countries benefit from the exchange of experience with experts and officials from non-Member economies.

The CCNM's programmes cover the major policy areas of OECD expertise that are of mutual interest to non-Members. These include: economic monitoring, structural adjustment through sectoral policies, trade policy, international investment, financial sector reform, international taxation, environment, agriculture, labour market, education and social policy, as well as innovation and technological policy development

Publié en français sous le titre :
EXAMENS DES POLITIQUES NATIONALES D'ÉDUCATION
Lettonie

Foreword

The transition of Latvia towards a pluralistic democracy and a market economy has been marked by economic, social and political changes of extraordinary breadth and depth. The talents, skills and knowledge base of the Latvian population are crucial in this process; hence the ambitious scale and urgency of the reforms being advanced for education. Education has been a central priority of the Baltic countries since regaining independence. As a small country with limited natural resources, Latvia sees its human capital as an important asset for eventual entry into the European Union and to compete in the global economy.

This Review offers a comprehensive picture of the significant progress in education reform since Latvia re-established independence. Changes have occurred in the contents of instruction (a new structure and content of curricula), the system of education, institutions (new types of education institutions, a redesigned schooling network) and education provision including new principles of the management and financing of the education system. The OECD examiners whose report forms the basis of this Review, however, concurred with the conclusions of the Government that, despite the progress, the reforms have not resulted from a comprehensive and publicly supported view on the architecture of the Latvian education system and its functioning. Problems have been addressed separately without the necessary co-ordination from the perspective of the whole education system. The Review offers advice on issues of access, equity, quality, the introduction of new technologies and decentralisation of management and financing responsibilities.

On the basis of background material prepared by the Latvian authorities and information supplied in meetings in the course of site visits, this Review provides an overview of education in the Baltic region and covers the entire system of Latvian education from pre-school through tertiary education and lifelong learning for all. The Review gives an analysis of these sectors in light of the economic, social and political context of Latvia. The final chapter, on strategic development, presents a synthesis of the examiners' specific recommendations and sets out how policies can and should be addressed system-wide, linked to priority issues of access and equity, quality, efficiency and governance.

3

This Review of Education Policy was undertaken within the framework of the Baltic Regional Programme of the OECD Centre for Co-operation with Non-Members (CCNM) and was financed through a grant from EC-Phare. Reviews of Estonia and Lithuania are forthcoming as publications in 2001. The conclusions and recommendations of the three country reviews were discussed at a special session of the Education Committee, hosted by Finland on 26 and 27 June 2000 in Helsinki and attended by the Ministers of Education of Estonia, Latvia and Lithuania. This report incorporates key points raised in the course of that discussion.

Members of the review team were: Aims McGuinness (United States), General Rapporteur, Johanna Crighton (The Netherlands), Gaby Hostens (Belgium), Pasi Sahlberg (Finland), Yael Duthilleul (World Bank), Hanna Autere and Hans-Konrad Koch (European Training Foundation) and Ian Whitman (Secretariat).

This volume is published on the responsibility of the Secretary-General of the OECD.

Eric Burgeat
Director
Centre for Co-operation with Non-Members

Table of Contents

Chapter 1

Context

Chapter 2

Latvian Education System

Chapter 3

Compulsory and General Education

Chapter 4

Vocational Education and Training

Chapter 5

Access and Equity for Latvian Children

Chapter 6

Higher Education

Chapter 7

Strategic Policy Development for Education in Latvia

Overview of Education Policy Reviews of Estonia, Latvia and Lithuania

Background of the Reviews

This review is one of three of education policy in the Baltic States conducted in 1999. These represent the most comprehensive reviews of education policy in each of these countries since they regained independence in 1991.

Methodology

The reviews were undertaken by three separate international teams composed of experts and high ranking officials drawn from OECD Member countries and Central and Eastern European States. The same rapporteur, however, participated in each review. Each country provided extensive background data and information. To complement the information gathered for these reviews and to avoid duplication, the OECD reviews drew upon reports of the World Bank, the United Nations Development Programme, the United Nations Children's Fund (UNICEF), the European Training Foundation and other European Union (EU) agencies, and the Soros Foundation as well as other non-governmental organisations. A 1999 OECD review of economic policy in the Baltic States also provided important background information for the education policy reviews.[1]

Importance of the reviews

Education has been a central priority of each of the Baltic States since they regained independence. It is critical to each country's transition from a half-century of Soviet occupation and pervasive impact of Soviet policy, ideology, and command economy. As small countries with limited natural resources, the Baltic States recognise that human capital is among their most important asset to compete in the global economy. All three Baltic States understand that progressive education and training policies are essential pre-requisites to accession to the European Union.

The OECD reviews are in-depth analyses of policy affecting all education levels and sectors – from early childhood and pre-school education through the doctoral level. While not a specific subject for review, the teams examined science policy as it interacts with higher education policy. Since education underpins the economic and social well being of all countries, the reviews addressed the links between education and other issues such as the status of women and children, regional economic development, and public administration reform.

The reviews were carried out at the specific request of national authorities. Each government recognised the value of the reviews to contribute to the national debate about the future of education policy and to raise important issues that it would be difficult for authorities within the country to raise.

The intent of an OECD review is not to evaluate a country's education policy but to place those policies in a comparative perspective. The Baltic States reviews emphasised both themes that cut across all three countries as well as issues that were unique to each country. Particular attention was given to:

- Identifying and respecting the unique geography, demography and economy of each state.

- Identifying good practice in policy and process that could be shared among the three countries and with other OECD Member and Non-Member states.

- Avoiding the uniform application of inappropriate policies to diverse problems.

The reviews focused in particular on the perspective of the state and the public interest and the interaction between state policy and institutions (providers), students/learners, and other clients of the education system (social partners, for example). These relationships are illustrated in Figure 1.

As in countries throughout the world, governments in the Baltic States have been shifting their focus from a primary concern for maintaining and supporting public institutions toward a greater emphasis on encouraging a wider range of providers (*e.g.*, private institutions) to serve student demand and public priorities. The governments are using public policy to ensure responsiveness of the education system to the needs of students/learners and social partners. The

OECD teams, therefore, sought to understand how these changes are taking place – and the developing policy issues related to the changes – in each of the Baltic States.

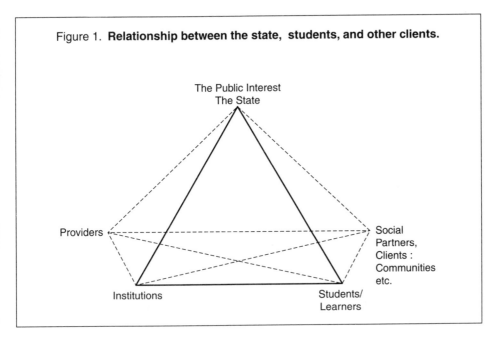

Figure 1. **Relationship between the state, students, and other clients.**

Similarities and differences among Baltic States

While Estonia, Latvia and Lithuania have a number of points in common, it is important to recognise points of difference that have a direct bearing on education policy.

Similarities

The following is a summary of important similarities:

- Through their early histories, all three countries experienced extended periods of conflict and domination by foreign powers, most notably the Order of Teutonic Knights, Tsarist Russia, German states, and Sweden, and in the case of Lithuania, Poland.

- In the aftermath of World War I, all three countries emerged from more than a century within the Russian Empire to gain independence and membership in the League of Nations. All three countries suffered severely in struggles among German, Russian and other forces in the course of World War I.

- In the initial period of independence, all three countries experienced a period of economic growth, improvement in the standard of living, and development of democratic institutions, although each experienced periods of political instability and threats to democratic institutions.

- All three countries were subjected to the secret conditions of the 1939 Mototov-Ribbentrop Pact between Nazi Germany and the Soviet Union that led to the stationing of Soviet troops and Soviet control in 1940, followed in June 1940 by Nazi invasion and German occupation until the closing months of World War II, when the Soviet Union regained control. During the alternative periods of Soviet and German occupation, hundreds of thousands of Latvians, Lithuanians, and Estonians were either killed or deported to Siberia, and hundreds of thousands of others escaped to other countries.

- All three countries experienced Stalin's brutality as the Soviet Union established control after World War II, including imprisonment and deportation of thousands to Siberia, forced immigration of Russian-speaking populations from the Soviet Union to work on collectivised farms and in large industries, suppression of religion, and imposition of Soviet ideological, military and economic controls.

- In almost 50 years of Soviet occupation, all three countries were subjected to the full force of Soviet ideological, political and economic policies as republics within the Soviet Union. To varying degrees, the Baltic States were afforded limited flexibility to adopt unique education policies reflecting language and culture, but in all other respects the countries were fully integrated into the Soviet Union.

- All three countries experienced a new awakening and drive for independence in the late 1980s in the climate of glasnost and perastroika, and the deterioration of Soviet institutions, culminating in the "Singing Revolution" and the re-establishment of independence in 1990 and 1991. (Lithuania re-established independence on March 11, 1990, Estonia on August 20, 1991, and Latvia on August 21, 1991.

- Upon re-establishing independence, all three countries reverted to Constitutions based largely upon those established in the initial period of independence after World War I.

- All three countries have moved aggressively to adopt progressive governmental, economic, social, and education reforms. All three countries have been accepted as candidates for accession to the European Union.

Differences

Several significant differences among the Baltic States, however, are especially important to an understanding of differences in education policy:

- All three countries had unique early histories and relations with other nations and cultures that have had lasting effects on culture and language and continue to influence national perspectives and policy. Lithuania has at times been linked to – and often has had contentious relations with - Poland over its history (Vilnius was part of Poland until World War II). Large parts of Estonia and Latvia were the country of Livonia until the mid-XVIth century. Latvia and Estonia have historically had closer ties with the Nordic countries than Lithuania – Estonia with Finland, Denmark and Sweden, and Latvia with Denmark and Sweden.

- Estonian, Latvian and Lithuanian are three highly distinct languages. Latvian and Lithuanian belong to the Baltic-branch of the Indo-European language family. Estonian belongs to the Finno-Ugric family of languages – along with Finnish, Hungarian, Udmurt, Sami, Komi, Mari, Livonian, and Mordvinian.

- Lithuania is a more ethnically homogeneous country than Estonia and Latvia. In 1999, Lithuanians comprised 81.3% of the populations, and Russians (8.4%) and Poles (7%) constituted the largest minority populations. In contrast, 55.7% of Latvia's population was Latvian and 32.2% were ethnic Russians. In Estonia, 65.2% were Estonians and 28.1% were ethnic Russians. The high percentage of ethnic Russians – especially in Estonia and Latvia – reflects the years of forced immigration, especially in the post-World War II period. Since re-establishment of independence, all three countries have experienced an out-migration of Russian populations, although out-migration has slowed considerably in recent years. Within Latvia and Estonia, the concentrations of ethnic Russian population tend to be in the major urban areas (Riga and Tallinn), and in regions associated with former Soviet industries or large collective farms.

- In Estonia and Latvia the largest religious group is Lutheran but in Lithuania it is Roman Catholic.

13

- All three countries are parliamentary republics in which the Government is headed by a Prime Minister appointed by the president, and a council (Latvia and Estonia) or cabinet (Latvia) of ministers, and a president who is head of state. In contrast to Estonia and Latvia where the president is elected by the parliament and plays a largely ceremonial role, the President of Lithuania is elected by popular election to a five-year term and has broader executive powers than the presidents of the other two countries.

- All three countries have pursued economic reforms to move dramatically from the command economy totally controlled by and oriented toward the Soviet Union, to market economies with increasingly strong relationships with Europe and the global economy. Each, however, has pursued independent economic policies with consequent differences in key economic indicators.[2]

Phases of Reform

Education reform in the Baltic States is best understood in terms of phases beginning in the late 1980s. Each country's reforms can be traced to initiatives in 1988 (if not earlier) undertaken in the spirit of the new awakening, perestroika, and the deterioration of Soviet institutions. In this period, each country experienced unprecedented grass roots engagement of educators in the exploration of new possibilities – initially within the Soviet Union, and then increasingly with the realisation that full re-establishment of independence was possible.

In the 1990-1992 period all three countries re-established independence and established Constitutions (based largely on earlier Constitutions) and the initial legal framework for education. Each country enacted a basic framework law, a Law on Education, for the education system. While each of these initial education laws reflects unique points for each country, the laws include common points regarding democratic principles, freedom from the ideological controls of the past, opportunities for private institutions, and significantly increased autonomy for universities. Enacted in the rapidly developing circumstances of 1991, these initial laws would require further refinement in later years.

In the 1992-1994 period, each of the Baltic States faced extraordinary challenges in gaining economic stability and establishing new legal frameworks and institutional structures. The economic dislocation in the collapse of the Soviet-oriented command economy and the slow development of new social and economic policies created severe hardships for each country's education systems. Nevertheless, each country continued to make progress on basic elements of education reform: eliminating ideologically oriented elements within universities, development of new curricula, textbooks, and teaching materials, and developing new links with Western donors and partners such as the Soros Foundation, the British Council, and the European Union Phare programme.

The 1995-1996 period brought a temporary pause in the positive developments since re-establishing independence as banking crises and economic instability drew attention and energy away from education reform. This was also a period in which the governments in each country attempted to shape new state policies to provide a degree of order and direction (e.g., through national curricula and standards) to the previously largely decentralised and often fragmented reforms.

In the 1996-1998 period, all three countries experienced their strongest periods of economic revitalisation and growth since 1991. In education reform, each country broadened the conceptual foundation for education reform and developed the second generation of legal frameworks for general education, vocational and professional education, and higher education. The Laws on Education first enacted in 1991-1992 were either replaced or amended significantly to reflect an increased maturity in each country's education reforms. Each country embarked on the development of new national curricula and assessment/testing policies, drawing on the expertise of foreign advisors and reflecting the best practice of many Western countries.

The Russian economic crisis beginning with the devaluation of the rouble on August 17th, 1998 slowed the economic growth as well as the pace of education reform of the previous two years in all three countries. This pause was clearly evident at the time of the site visits for the OECD reviews in 1999. Yet the commitment to reform remained strong as evidenced by continued progress on national curricula, new assessment policies, development of new textbooks and teaching materials, and enactment of new laws for non-university higher education ("colleges"). The countries continued to make progress on higher education reform through continued strengthening of the capacity of universities to accommodate escalating demand and the international expectations for quality in academic programmes and research.

Conceptual foundation for reform

As mentioned above, all three countries adopted framework Laws on Education in 1991 (Lithuania and Latvia) and 1992 (Estonia) that included similar concepts and principles. At the same time, each country pursued a different path in the development of a conceptual foundation for education reform.

Lithuania provides the clearest example of the development of a basic document, the 1992 General Concept of Education in Lithuania, which has served as the foundation of education reform and legislation throughout the pre- and post-independence periods. The Concept sets out four phases: phase I from the end of 1988 to March 11, 1990; phase II leading to the framing of the Concept in 1992; and phases III and IV (1992 to 2005) during which "a uniform, permanent Lithuanian educational system is created covering formal and informal education and an expanded network of public and private educational institutions."

In both Estonia and Latvia, the development of a broadly accepted conceptual foundation for education reform has been more of an evolving process. In Estonia, for example, not until the late 1990s did a broad consensus emerge around the concept "Learning Estonia", developed by the Academic Council convened by the President of the Republic of Estonia, "Estonian Education Strategy" compiled by the Ministry of Education and "Estonian Education Scenarios 2015" designed by the task force of the Committee of the Education Forum. In Latvia, the Ministry of Education and Science developed a "Latvian Concept of Education" in 1995, but from the observations of the OECD team, this document did not receive wide acceptance as the foundation for reform. Nevertheless, despite changes in governments, Latvian education reform has evolved on the basis of an informal consensus about the principles that should guide the country's education system.

In their reports, the OECD review teams emphasised the importance of a broad understanding of and commitment to the principles of education reform as an essential condition for sustained progress and for translating concepts into strategies and actions – especially in the case of frequent changes in political leadership. Such an understanding and commitment must reach not only to all levels of the education system but also to the nation's political and civic leadership and social partners. Whether or not the conceptual foundation is reflected in a formal document, all three countries face the challenge of engaging the society as a whole in the process of change.

Common themes

Despite the clear differences among Estonia, Latvia, and Lithuania, the OECD teams observed a number of common themes in education policy shared by all three countries. These can be divided between sector-specific themes and those that cut across all sectors.

Sector-specific themes

All three countries are engaged in reform of each level and sector of their education systems from pre-school through higher education. The issues identified by the OECD teams most often related to the points of inter-section or transition. Examples include:

- The inter-section between education and broader social and economic problems such as the relationship of pre-school education to the health and welfare of young children and women, and the relationship of vocational education to the changing economy and labour market.

- The transition between pre-school education and compulsory education and policies to ensure that all young children are prepared and ready to learn.

- The transition between compulsory education and upper-secondary education and policies designed to ensure that a wider range of students complete compulsory education with the depth and breadth of academic preparation to pursue further education or to enter the labour market – and to continue learning throughout their lifetimes.

- The transition between upper secondary general and professional/vocational education (grades 10 through 12) and either the labour market or higher education.

The following are highlights of the themes related to the major sectors.

Strengthening Pre-school/ Early Childhood Education

In all three countries, pre-school enrolment dropped precipitously following independence as the countries moved away from the extensive network of pre-school establishments linked to Soviet-era working places. The need to ensure that all young children are prepared for compulsory education is a shared concern, but the approaches being taken to address the issues differ. At the time of the OECD review, Lithuania was moving to lower the age of the beginning of compulsory education from age 7 to include children in "zero" level classes (generally 6-year olds). Latvia extended compulsory education to include pre-school education in the Law on Education enacted in 1998 but repealed this provision (primarily for economic reasons) in 1999. Estonia is taking steps to strengthen pre-school education including strengthening the requirements for teacher preparation and establishing new financing policies. The OECD reviews strongly supported the initiatives to achieve the goal of ensuring that all young children are prepared to enter school, but the teams raised concerns about the adequacy of resources, training of teachers and other support – especially in rural areas – to make this goal a reality. Another common concern is that there should be strong links between state initiatives aimed at improving the health and welfare of young children and women and policies related to pre-school education. In some cases, the responsibility for these inter-related areas is divided among different ministries.

Strengthening (extending) compulsory education and improving the quality of education for all students

Reform of compulsory education has been a central focus of education reform in all three Baltic States since the late 1980s. All countries moved rapidly to "de-ideologise" the curriculum and to establish the basis and transition process (curriculum, textbooks, and curricular materials, and retraining of teachers) for education systems in which the language of instruction was primarily in the national language (Estonian, Latvian, or Lithuanian). In the initial years, reform was largely a grass-roots phenomenon with great variation throughout the countries in the extent and direction of change. Multiple well-intentioned but often unco-ordinated foreign initiatives and pilots both stimulated reform and contributed indirectly to the lack of coherence in education reform. By the mid-1990s, however, each country moved to develop national curricula and standards and began the process of developing quality assurance mechanisms such as centrally set and/or administered assessments and examinations. The countries faced – and continue to face – a number of common problems:

- Refining the initial assessment and testing instruments to ensure that they reflect the goals of national curricula such as integration of knowledge and practice and active learning.

- Narrowing the gap between the goals of reform and the realities of change at the classroom and school levels including the need for basic instructional materials, teacher in-service education, and other support.

- Increasing the coherence in the often-fragmented provision of teacher in-service education and a stronger link of the available programmes to implementation of new curriculum and assessment policies.

- Undertaking fundamental reform of pre-service teacher education to reflect the principles of education reform.

- Ensuring quality across diverse systems.

- Addressing the problems of small rural schools and severe differences between urban and rural areas in the quality and cost-effectiveness of schools.

With the assistance of the Soros Foundation and Phare and other external assistance, the Baltic States have made impressive progress in extending the application of information technology (ICT), especially access to computers and the Internet, throughout their education systems, but especially in compulsory/general education. Estonia's Tiger Leap initiative, for example, which began as a commitment to ensure that all students had access to computers, has evolved into a far broader initiative aimed at ensuring that Estonians are prepared to thrive and compete in the global information economy.

Reforming post-compulsory education (upper secondary education)

Many of the issues that relate to compulsory education (*e.g.* curriculum, standards, quality assurance, and teacher training) were also evident at the post-compulsory (upper-secondary) level. A basic challenge faced by all three countries is to provide a larger proportion of each post-compulsory age cohort with a broader general education within either general secondary education schools (gymnasiums) or secondary vocational education. In Soviet times, many academically weaker students entered vocational schools directly following compulsory education to be trained for narrowly defined working places in state-owned enterprises. Only limited general education was included in that training. Other students entered secondary vocational schools to prepare for specialised technical fields that required a broader general education foundation but generally did not prepare students further education at the university level, although some students continued in specialised post-secondary education training.

With the collapse of the command economy linked to the Soviet Union, the state enterprises for which vocational schools trained students ceased to exist. A combination of low-prestige and outdated training programmes, equipment and teachers contributed to a precipitous decline in demand for secondary vocational education.

The pattern in the post-independence period in all three Baltic countries has been to lengthen the period of general education for all students and to delay specialisation. An increasing proportion of those completing compulsory education is seeking to enter general secondary education – and, if possible, more highly selective gymnasiums – which will increase the chances for university entrance. At the same time, vocational secondary education is converging with

19

general secondary education, as countries are developing new national standards and examinations for grade 12 that all students much complete – whether in general or vocational secondary education. The increased demand for vocational education is at the post-secondary level for students who have completed secondary education and seek specialised training to enter the labour market.

Common developments across the three countries include:

• Continuing development of national curricula and standards;

• Implementation of externally developed and administered grade 12 examinations;

• Gaining acceptance of universities of the use of grade 12 examinations for university entrance (this is in place in Estonia and under consideration in Lithuania and Latvia);

• Diversifying upper secondary education through "profiling" (Lithuania) and other changes in the curriculum to accommodate a wider range of student abilities and aspirations.

Reforming vocational education and training

As described above, the vocational education and training systems of all three countries were closely tied to the Soviet command economy. Outdated curricula, obsolete equipment and training materials, deteriorating facilities, and teachers who were ill-prepared for new professions and market economy combined to make the vocational education and training systems largely irrelevant to the developing labour market.

All three Baltic countries have made important progress in reform of vocational education and training over the decade of the 1990s – stimulated by the goal of EU accession and supported by foreign assistance. The EC Phare programme and the European Training Foundation (ETF) have played significant, positive roles in developing conceptual and strategic basis for reform, and in supporting pilot programmes in areas such as curriculum development, regional training and development, and teacher training. In the 1997-99 period, all three countries completed work on and enacted new framework laws on vocational education and training. These new laws establish national qualification systems, provide for extensive involvement of social partners at every level, clarify the roles of different schools, establish new non-university sectors (ISCED 4B and 5B), and strengthen the links between vocational education and training and regional economic development. Common issues faced by all three countries included:

- Moving from concepts and strategies to concrete actions. While the basic legal framework and formal policy structures are in place, all three countries need to accelerate implementation of concrete reforms. Foreign assistance has been an indispensable catalyst for reform, but implementing and sustaining reform will require stronger leadership and funding from the countries themselves.

- Establishing state leadership structures for co-ordination of vocational education and training across all ministries. Estonia and Lithuania have recently transferred responsibility for agricultural vocational education and training institutions from the Ministry of Agriculture to the Ministry of Education with the result most vocational training institutions are now under a single ministry. In Latvia, responsibility for these institutions continues to be shared by several ministries, although the Ministry of Education and Science has overall co-ordinating responsibility. Developing effective co-ordination between the state vocational education system and state employment services – the entity responsible for labour market information, short-term training of the unemployed, and regional labour market services under the jurisdiction of another ministry – remains an issue in all three countries.

- Optimising the school network. All three countries face the problem of two many small, highly specialised vocational schools. Each is taking actions to close or merge schools and to modernise and broaden the profiles of other schools. In some instances, secondary vocational schools, or technicums, are evolving into "colleges" at the ISCED 4B level and being linked with other institutions to form complexes that are more cost-effective.

- Clarifying the roles of the developing "colleges". The development of post-secondary institutions at the non-university level is evolving in each of the countries, yet there remains a degree of ambiguity about the role and mission of these new institutions. All the vocational education and training reforms have emphasised the need for a new sector at the non-university level to train highly skilled technicians for the developing labour market. All the reforms emphasise that these institutions should relate "horizontally" to the labour market and should be closely linked with social partners. When fully developed, such institutions should also provide an alternative to university-level education. Essentially two kinds of institutions are developing. First, institutions at the post-secondary level evolving from former "technicums" but not oriented toward preparation for university entrance (ISCED 1997 4B); and second, colleges offering university-level professional programmes (ISCED 1997 5B) that are more clearly linked to universities and, in some cases, are governed by universities. In part because the demand in the labour market for specialists trained at the ISCED 4B and 5B levels is still developing, many of the students attending these institutions still aspire primarily to pursue a university education rather than enter the labour market following training. The potential proliferation of new post-secondary or higher education institutions raises fundamental policy questions about quality assurance and financing for all three countries.

- Engaging social partners. The development of stronger roles for social partners in the reform of vocational education and training is a clear need in all three countries. Participation of social partners is needed in the new national qualification systems, advising in the design of training programmes, providing apprenticeship and other work-site training, and providing up-to-date equipment and training materials.

- Training of vocational education teachers. The retraining of current teachers and training of new teachers is a major need throughout the Baltic States.

Reforming tertiary education

All three Baltic States have made great strides in restructuring their higher education system since the major changes began in 1988. Changes included:

- Instilling democratic principles and processes throughout the universities.

- Establishing a new legal framework providing for institutions of higher education, university autonomy, a new research infrastructure, the framework for quality assurance, and a differentiated higher education system.

- Eliminating previous restrictions in content and pedagogy, especially in the social sciences and humanities, and eliminating required military retraining as a compulsory part of the curriculum.

- Carrying out dramatic shifts in academic programmes in response to changing student demands and the economic reality of the need to generate additional revenue from fee-paying students to offset limitations in state funding.

- Moving from the narrow Soviet degree structure to an award structure that is not only more flexible but also consistent with Western models and increasing expectations (*e.g.*, Bologna) for common structures across Europe and the world.

- Abolishing the academies of science as research organisations, reconstituting the academies as honorary societies, and integrating research into the universities, resulting in substantial gains in research and greatly strengthened universities.

- Strengthening graduate education, especially through the integration of research and teaching at the doctoral level in contrast to the location of doctoral programmes outside the universities in Soviet times.

At the time of the OECD reviews, there was growing recognition that further changes in higher education policies would be necessary. In Lithuania, for example, a new Law on Institutions of Higher Education in Lithuania was under consideration. Major issues remaining at the time of the reviews included:

- Accommodating the escalating demand for university-level education, including alternatives such as non-university "colleges".

- Tightening quality assurance requirements, including stronger requirements for non-public institutions.

- Reforming the financing of higher education, including the highly sensitive issue of student fees.

- Conforming degree structures to international expectations as defined by the Bologna Joint Declaration.

- Developing new modes of delivery including open-distance learning and greatly expanded use of information technology throughout the higher education system.

- Seeking solutions, including strengthened doctoral programmes and international affiliations, to the problem of retraining current professors and developing the next generation of faculty and researchers.

23

• Reforming university programmes for teacher education.

Having granted universities substantial autonomy at the time of re-esta-blishing independence, all three countries are now debating ways to increase the responsiveness of higher education institutions to public priorities and to ensu-re greater public accountability. At the time of the OECD reviews, each country was debating measures that would provide for a stronger role for the State in set-ting priorities while enhancing the quality, responsiveness and international competitiveness of the universities and other higher education institutions.

Strengthening adult education and lifelong learning

The Baltic states face a common need to prepare their adult populations to participate in democratic society and a market economy, and to continue to learn and adjust to the dramatic changes occurring in the technology-intensive global economy. Nevertheless, the institutional network remains largely oriented to stu-dents who have recently completed compulsory or upper secondary education and is not effectively linked or co-ordinated with the labour market training network.

All three countries have expressed policy commitments to lifelong learning and established new legal frameworks for adult education, but a major challen-ge remains to translate these policies into concrete implementation. New deve-lopments in the use of information technology and open-distance learning (open universities) show promise as means to provide access for the adult population to further education and training. As the economies develop, employers should play an increasing role in the demand for accessible training opportunities. Other providers – primarily non-public institutions – are responding to the need, but these programmes tend to be in areas where the demand and potential for economic gain are greatest (business, law, and foreign languages) and are avai-lable primarily in the urban areas. State policies for regulating quality continue to be weak and the cost of non-public programmes makes them inaccessible to large segments of the adult population.

Crosscutting themes

As reflected in the summary of sector-specific themes, the OECD teams iden-tified a number of crosscutting themes that are evident in all three Baltic States.

Strengthening and sustaining national policy leadership for education reform

Frequent changes in governments and ministers of education have created serious problems for all three Baltic States in sustaining national policy leadership for education reform. In face of this instability, the countries have benefited from a general consensus within education networks and among major political parties and non-governmental organisations (NGOs) about the conceptual foundations and goals of education reform. External forces, such as the expectations established for accession to the EU, have played a key role in sustaining reform. Within the constraints of leadership changes, limited resources, and under-developed civil service laws, all three countries have made progress in reforming the roles and functioning of the ministries of education. Common goals of these reforms include:

- Shifting the oversight and quality assurance emphasis from controlling and inspecting "inputs" (*e.g.*, detailed curriculum and curriculum timetables), toward overseeing the accomplishment of "outcomes" while allowing schools and institutions greater independence in shaping the details of implementation.

- Strengthening the professional qualifications of ministry personnel.

- Emphasising decentralisation and deregulation.

- Strengthening the ministry capacity for strategic planning and policy leadership.

- Increasing the co-ordination between government initiatives and initiatives supported by NGOs and foreign sponsors.

Despite these promising developments, the OECD teams observed that all three countries face a challenge in broadening and deepening the commitment of society – especially political leaders and social partners – to education reform as a fundamental foundation for essentially all the countries' major policy goals. The countries also all face the challenge of sustaining attention to education reform across the inevitable changes in government. The specific mechanism for addressing these challenges will be different in each country, but the leadership must come from the highest levels of government and will likely require extensive use of non-governmental organisations that can provide for continuity when government cannot do so.

As mentioned at several points in this overview, EC Phare, the Soros Foundation, and other foreign sponsors have provided invaluable stimulus and support for education reform in all three Baltic States. Foreign assistance is not a satisfactory long-term substitute for permanent, sustained leadership within each country. The OECD teams were concerned that, as foreign-supported pilot projects

25 |

and NGOs phase out their support in critical areas such as reform of vocational education and training, the commitment and capacity to sustain reform may not exist.

Narrowing the gap between concepts/strategies and the realities of practice and implementation

All three countries have developed essential legal and policy frameworks. However, in large part because of the instability in national leadership, the countries face significant problems in moving to practical application. This is especially evident in the general secondary and vocational education and training systems in which a significant gap remains between the reform goals and the realities of change at the level of the school and classroom. The national leaders expressed concern about this gap in the course of the OECD reviews and all three countries will be giving more attention to the basic infrastructure and support systems necessary to deepen the impact of reform. Greater emphasis on alignment of teacher pre-service and in-service education and training of school directors with reform goals are examples of such efforts. As mentioned above, developing the commitment and capacity to assume responsibility and sustain initiatives originated through foreign sponsors will be especially important in bridging the gap between strategy and practice.

Addressing concerns about equity and fairness

All three Baltic States have made strong commitments to civil liberties and to narrowing the gaps in access and opportunity for all people within their countries. They recognise that fulfilling these commitments is an essential condition for modern democracies, for accession to the European Union, and for full participation in the global economy. In the OECD education policy reviews, the teams underscored the need for further progress on:

- Narrowing the disparities in quality and educational opportunity between urban and rural areas (including the need for public administration reform to address the problems of small municipalities that lack the capacity to sustain strong schools).

- Ensuring that special needs students are served, including addressing the health and economic needs of young children to ensure that they are ready to learn.

- Continuing to make progress on addressing the needs of language and ethnic minority populations to ensure that they can be full participants in the civic and economic life of the countries.

- Countering the strong tendencies toward elite secondary schools and a focus on university entrance with deliberate steps to ensure that all students – not only the most academically gifted and those with social and economic advantages – have access to quality education and the opportunity to gain essential knowledge and skills.

Recognising the impact of government reform on education policy

In the course of the education policy reviews, the OECD teams were repeatedly reminded that the progress of education reform often depends on reform of other areas of government. As examples:

- Resolution of questions of public administration reform will have a direct impact on the progress of education reform. While the specific legal and financial responsibilities of municipalities for education differ among the three countries, each faces the problem of small rural municipalities that lack the capacity to fulfil their education responsibilities. Each of the Baltic States faces fundamental issues related to the structure, roles, and financing of municipal governments and about appropriate roles and responsibilities of entities between municipalities and the national government (regions, counties, or other entities).

- Reforming civil services policies. Civil service reform across all levels of government is a critical prerequisite for strengthening the policy leadership, analytic, oversight, and support functions of ministries of education and other governmental units responsible for education.

- Aligning state finance policies with education reform. In each of the Baltic States, the ministry of finance plays a critical and often dominant role in education policy, yet, from the observations of the OECD review teams, these policies are not always consistent with or supportive of education reform goals. The issues are not only on the level of state financing of education, but also on the details of policy implementation. As emphasised earlier, continued progress in education reform will require leadership and co-ordination at the highest level of government and across all ministries with responsibilities that have an impact on education.

Conclusion

The human resources of Estonia, Latvia and Lithuania are these countries' most valuable assets. As small countries with comparatively limited natural resources, the Baltic States' future will depend on the knowledge and skills of their people. Education of all the people, not only young children and youth but also adults, should be each nation's highest priority.

The Baltic States have made extraordinary progress in education reform over the past decade. The OECD teams were especially impressed by the dedication of teachers, professors, school directors and university leaders who, despite exceptionally difficult times, have persevered, maintained quality, and led the way in changes necessary to prepare students for participation in democracy and a market economy. The OECD teams are confident that the leaders in each of the countries have the vision and commitment to ensure continued progress in education reform into the XXIst century.

Notes

1. OECD, OECD Economic Surveys: The Baltic States, A Regional Economic Assessment. Paris: OECD, 2000.

2. See OECD, The Baltic States, A Regional Economic Assessment.

Chapter 1

Context

Geography

With a territory of 64 600 sq. km, Latvia lies on the Eastern coast of the Baltic sea and shares borders with Estonia in the North, Russia and Belarus in the East and Lithuania in the South. The Baltic Sea connects Latvia also with Sweden, Finland, Germany and Denmark. This location has traditionally made Latvia an important transit route between Europe and Russia. This was especially the case during the period of the Hanseatic League, but Latvia remains a strong transit economy for the movement of oil and other products from Russia to ports such as Ventspils. Less than one-half of the country is arable. Woodlands cover 44% of the territory and are an important source of timber. The country has few natural resources and imports all its natural gas and oil products, and half of its electricity needs.

The three largest sectors of the economy in terms of percentage of Gross Domestic Product (GDP) in year 1998 are manufacturing (17.9 % of GDP and 18.2% of employment); transport, storage and communications (16.7% of GDP and 8.1% of employment); and wholesale and retail trade (16.8% of GDP and 15.1% of employment). The highest percentage of employment is in agriculture, hunting and forestry (4.1% of GDP and 17% of employment).

There are 26 districts (*rajons*) and seven major cities in Latvia. Latvia is divided into four historic regions – Kurzeme, Vidzeme, Zemgale and Latgale, although these regions are not used as sub-national governmental jurisdictions. The map below shows the 26 *rajons* and the four historical regions of Latvia.

History

Latvia's history, especially in the 20th century, has significant implications for the status and future challenges of the Republic's education policy. Latvia

29

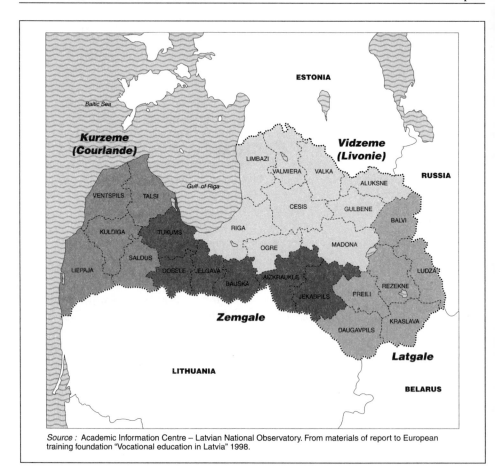

Source : Academic Information Centre – Latvian National Observatory. From materials of report to European training foundation "Vocational education in Latvia" 1998.

shares with Estonia and Lithuania the experience of independence in the period between World War I and World War II, the devastating events of World War II, and the subsequent period of Soviet control. In contrast to other countries in Eastern and Central Europe, the Baltic States were fully integrated with the Soviet Union. Consequently, these states were subjected to the full force of Soviet military and economic policies and the highly centralised education policies dictated from Moscow. A brief review of the 20th century is therefore important to an understanding of policies for the 21st century.

In 1201, German Teutonic knights conquered Latvia. By the 1270s, the crusaders had established the state of Livonia, a political union of territories belonging to the Livonian Order of Knights and to the Catholic church, covering the homelands of the Couronians, Semgallians, Latgallians, Selonians and Finno-

Ugrians (Estonians and Livs) in the territory of present-day Latvia and Estonia. After the Livonian Wars (1558-1583), Livonia was divided between Sweden and Poland-Lithuania. In 1704, Latvia was partially under the Russian Empire and in 1772, Russia annexed it. Latvian national independence became a public cause in the early years of the 20th century. In the Revolution of 1905, the struggle in Latvia was for social and political liberation against both German landowners and the Russian policy of national oppression. World War I (1914-18) crippled Latvia economically as the German army occupied the western half of the country. Fifty thousand of Latvia's 2.5 million inhabitants became refugees, while most of Latvia's industry was moved to the Russian interior. The division of the territory and economic hardships stimulated a sense of national identity and the drive for independence. On November 18, 1918, the Latvian People's Council for the first time proclaimed the national independence of the Republic of Latvia. The international community recognised Latvia's independence on January 26, 1921, and nine months later, Latvia was admitted to the League of Nations. During the period between the two World Wars, the country experienced considerable economic growth and an improvement in its standard of living during the 1930s.

The Baltic States suffered immeasurably during World War II by being caught between Nazi Germany and the Soviet Union. On August 23, 1939, Latvia and Estonia (and subsequently, Lithuania) were illegally placed under Soviet control in the secret protocols of the Nazi-Soviet Non-Aggression Pact (the Molotov-Ribbentrop Pact). Latvia was forced to grant military bases to the Soviet Union in September 1939, and on June 17, 1940 Soviet troops invaded. During the night of June 13-14, 1941, tens of thousands of Latvia's inhabitants were deported to Siberia. Then, on June 22, 1941, despite Hitler's assurances to Stalin that he would not invade Russia, Hitler launched a massive attack on Russia and German forces invaded Latvia. German occupation lasted until 1944, when the Soviet troops returned. After World War II, Soviet rule was re-established, though not recognised by most Western states.[1]

By the end of the war, Latvia had lost one-third of its population. Between 110 000 and 120 000 individuals were imprisoned, deported to Soviet camps, or killed. An estimated 130 000 fled to the West. The post-World War II period from 1944 until Stalin's death in 1953 was especially harsh for Latvia. On March 25, 1949, 43 000 people were deported from Latvia to Siberia. A massive campaign followed of deportations and mass imprisonment, together with forced mass immigration of Russian-speaking non-natives to work in collectivised farms and large industries. The Soviet period significantly changed Latvia's population make-up. Before Soviet occupation in 1940, Latvians made up approximately 75% of the population, but by 1989, this figure was 52%.

The second national awakening began in the late 1980s following glasnost and perestroika. In 1988, a Popular Front for Latvia was formed and, in 1989, it won the elections to the Supreme Council. In 1990, the Supreme Council adopted a declaration renewing Latvia's independence. In 1990 and 1991 there were violent clashes between supporters of independence and Latvian communists and Soviet forces. A referendum in March 1991 voted 73% in favour of independence. On August 21, 1991, the Parliament in Latvia voted to re-establish de facto independence, restoring Latvia's pre-war status as a sovereign independent country. The Soviet Union recognised Latvian independence the following month. Russian military forces withdrew from the country in 1994.[2]

Demography

In the beginning of 1999, the population of Latvia was 2 439 445. Severe economic conditions, out-migration, and a natural decrease in population have contributed to a steady decline in Latvia's population over the past decade. In the period from 1990 to 1992, Latvia experienced a net out-migration of 111 000. Although the net outflow continues, it is now at a much slower pace. The major crisis is in underlying demographic trends, especially the declining birth rate. The natural birth rate has been decreasing since 1987. In 1991 it turned negative with the death rate exceeding births by 116 persons. In 1996, the population was 188 000 less than in 1991. In 1997, the death rate exceeded the birth rate in all the towns and regions. The changes in birth and mortality rates from 1986 to 1999 are shown in Figure 2.[3]

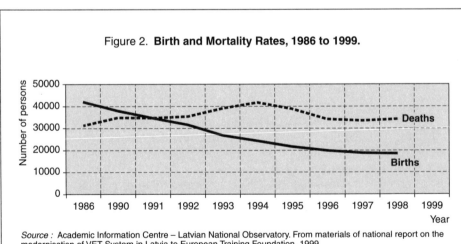

Figure 2. **Birth and Mortality Rates, 1986 to 1999.**

Source : Academic Information Centre – Latvian National Observatory. From materials of national report on the modernisation of VET System in Latvia to European Training Foundation, 1999.

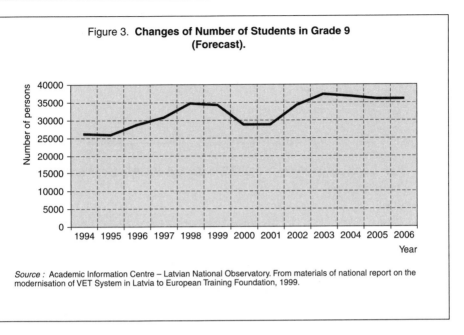

Figure 3. **Changes of Number of Students in Grade 9 (Forecast).**

Source : Academic Information Centre – Latvian National Observatory. From materials of national report on the modernisation of VET System in Latvia to European Training Foundation, 1999.

Latvia's school-aged population is shrinking rapidly (Figure 3). Between 1990 and 1998 the number of children born annually fell by 52% from 37 918 in 1990 to 18 410 in 1998. The birth rate (births per thousand population) declined from 14.2 in 1990 to 7.5 in 1998. The rate of decline in the number of births was initially much greater in the seven largest cities, but since 1994 the rate of decline in rural areas has outdistanced urban areas. The number of births fell by more than 48% in all *rajons* and cities between 1990 and 1996. In five of twenty-six *rajons* and two of the seven major cities, the decline was more than 60%. The decline in the birth rate can be attributed to the severe economic conditions, a change in social values of women regarding childbearing, and other variables.

It is difficult to anticipate the long-term impact of these demographic trends on the demand for education. For example, despite the likely decrease in demand because of declining birth rates, in the short-term the demand for secondary education will actually increase. Reflecting fluctuations in the birth rate in the 1980s, the number of students completing basic education at Grade 9 has been increasing in the late 1990s. That number is projected to decrease for the years of 2000 and 2001, and then increase again in the early 2000s.[4]

The population is ageing, thereby increasing the burden on younger age cohorts to support pensioners (Figure 4). In 1999, the share of the population eligible for pensions was 22.5%; the proportion of children and teenagers was 18.5.

One-third of Latvia's population (796 737 in the beginning of 1999) is located in the largest city and capital, Riga. Another 27% of the population is in the six relatively large cities with 40 000 to 120 000 inhabitants.[5] Nineteen percent of the population lives in smaller towns with fewer than 40 000 inhabitants, which Latvia classifies as urban areas. The total urban population is about 69% (Figure 5).

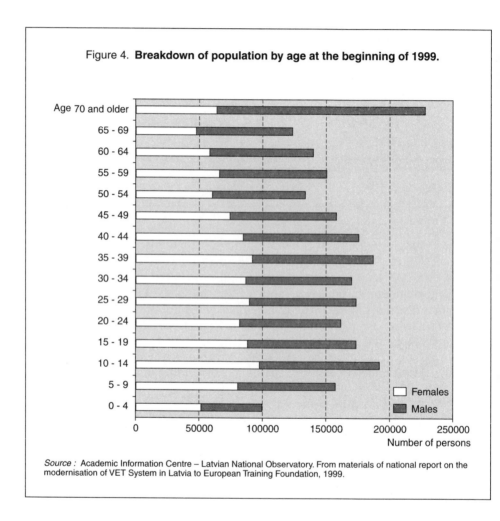

Figure 4. **Breakdown of population by age at the beginning of 1999.**

Source : Academic Information Centre – Latvian National Observatory. From materials of national report on the modernisation of VET System in Latvia to European Training Foundation, 1999.

Significant disparities exist between urban and rural areas (especially between Riga and other regions) in terms of economy, quality of life, and educational opportunities. In a review of data on poverty in Latvia, the UN Human

Development Programme in 1997 found that poverty is more widespread in rural areas than in urban areas, but is quite evenly spread across all four of Latvia's historic regions. However, in Latgale only 24.9% of the population spends more than the subsistence minimum. This underscores that this region has critical social problems requiring urgent attention. In contrast, relatively fewer people in the Riga region (Riga City and surrounding areas) were living below the poverty line.[6] Because in any country there is a clear link between poverty and education – both in terms of opportunity and quality – such disparities are an educational policy issue as well as a socio-economic one.

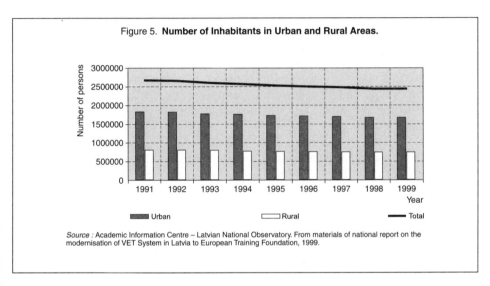

Figure 5. **Number of Inhabitants in Urban and Rural Areas.**

Source : Academic Information Centre – Latvian National Observatory. From materials of national report on the modernisation of VET System in Latvia to European Training Foundation, 1999.

Ethnic and language distribution

In the beginning of 1999, the ethnic distribution of Latvia's population was 55.7% Latvians, 32.3 Russians, 3.9% Belorussians, 2.9% Ukrainians, 2.2% Poles, 1.3% Lithuanians, and 1.7% other ethnic groups. The Russian population is heavily concentrated in Riga and major urban areas as well as in Southeast Latvia, and constitutes a majority of the population in these areas. Data on ethnicity do not necessarily reflect linguistic differences (there is significant overlap; for example, Latvians whose language is Russian or Russians whose language is Latvian; also, about 120 000 people use both languages in the home).[7]

Governmental structure

Latvia is a parliamentary republic first established on November 18, 1918. When Latvia regained its independence in August 1991, it declared the primacy

35

of the 1922 Constitution, or *Satversme*, over all laws in force in the country. After various amendments designed to establish parliamentary democracy, the Constitution was restored in its entirety in 1993. The Head of State in Latvia is the President elected by the *Saeima* (Parliament) for a period of four years. H.E. Mrs. Vaira Vike-Freiberga was elected President of the Republic of Latvia on June 17, 1999. The highest legislative body in Latvia is the one-chamber *Saeima* composed of 100 deputies and elected in direct, proportional elections by citizens 18 years of age and over. Deputies serve for four years and parties must receive at least 5% of the national vote to gain seats in the *Saeima*.

The President of the Republic designates the Prime Minister, who appoints the ministers. Law fixes the number of ministers – 12 at present. The ministers are also individually accountable to the *Saeima*. The Cabinet of Ministers holds executive power. On July 16, 1999, the *Saeima* voted to support the Cabinet headed by Andris Skele. The government is made up of the three parties (People's Party, Latvia's Way and For Fatherland and Freedom/LNNK). The government does not include the New Party, the National Harmony Party and the Latvian Social Democratic Alliance.

Latvia has not introduced any intermediate levels of government. The government is therefore obliged to negotiate directly with each local authority concerning issues that may affect the authority.

Latvia has 483 local municipalities (pagasts) organised in 26 regions (*rajons*), and 7 metropolitan cities. Each local authority has a Council elected by direct universal suffrage. The role of the *rajons* is limited and related to co-ordinating measures taken by the municipalities in the planning and management of local public services.

Economy

In the period from independence in 1918 to annexation by the Soviet Union in 1940, Latvia evolved an economy that was highly integrated with the West. Following World War II, central planning was introduced and Latvia became totally dependent on the Soviet Union for resources and distribution of finished products. The condition of the Latvian economy followed that of the Soviet Union. As the Soviet economy grew, so did Latvia's; but as the Soviet economy declined in later years, Latvia's economy also suffered.

Although Latvia instituted reforms in the late 1980s, dramatic changes did not occur until after renewed independence in 1991. Until the late 1980s, Latvia was a pure command economy, without a significant private sector.

With the abandonment of a command economy and the collapse of the Soviet Union, Latvia's Gross Domestic Product (GDP) declined by 50% from 1990 to 1993. In the following years, the economic situation stabilised. Except for a banking crisis in 1995, Latvia has made steady progress in the transition from a command to a market economy, while re-establishing the institutions of an independent state.

In mid-1999, the macroeconomic situation in Latvia was relatively stable. Despite the changes in government, the commitment remained to consistent economic and fiscal policy. Inflation continued to decline. Real GDP registered high growth in 1997, at the rate of 8.6%, but dropped to 3.9% in 1998. Unemployment increased to 9.2% in late 1998 (Table 1).

The slower increase in GDP and increased unemployment can be attributed largely to significantly reduced demand from Russia following the August 1998 Russian economic crisis. The devaluation of the ruble in August 1998 and the Russian financial crisis had a significant impact on Latvia because it decreased export opportunities. At the same time, however, Latvia has been reorienting its economy and decreasing its dependence on exports to Russia. Before regaining independence, Latvia had no trade relations outside the former socialist block. By 1998, more than half the Latvian trade turnover was with countries in the European Union. In October 1998, Latvia was the first of the Baltic States to be accepted into the World Trade Organisation.[8]

The structure of the economy continues to change dramatically, especially in those sectors associated with the previous economy and trade with the Russian Federation. Agriculture and heavy industry continue to decline, while the service sector is growing rapidly. From 1995 to 1998, agriculture, hunting and forestry decreased from 10.4% of GDP to 4.1% of GDP. Manufacturing decreased from 22.4% to 17.9% of GDP. In the same period, services increased from 56.0% to 65.4% of GDP. The most significant increases were in wholesale and retail trades from 11.3% to 16.8% of GDP; nevertheless transport, storage and communications increased from 16.0% to 16.7% of GDP.

Living standards and employment

Despite progress in recent years, the social and economic conditions for people in Latvia remain comparatively low. A substantial number of people continue to live in poverty. The Human Development Index (HDI) calculated by the United Nations Development Programme Latvia in 1999 placed Latvia in the 74th position in the world compared to 1998 (92nd position for Latvia, 77th position for Estonia and 79th position for Lithuania).[10] Household budget survey data from the Central Statistical Bureau in 1997 indicated that two-thirds of the residents of the state lived under the crisis subsistence minimum. This minimum was 56 lats per month compared to the average wage of 129.99 lats for people in the national economy in the first nine months of 1998. Most poor households had children and were unemployed. Disparities in wealth continue to grow. Income inequality as measured by the Gini Index[11] , an indicator of income distribution, increased slightly from 0.30 in 1996 to 0.31 in 1997 and 0.32 in 1998.[12]

Table 1. **Main Economic Indicators**
1994-1999

Indicator	1994	1995	1996	1997	1998	1999*
Real GDP Growth (%)	0.6	-0.8	3.3	8.6	3.6	0.1
Inflation rate (annual average (%)	35.9	25.0	17.6	8.4	4.7	2.4
Unemployment end of year, ILO definition[9] (%)		18.9	18.3	14.4	14.0	14.5
Registered unemployed (%)	6.5	6.6	7.2	7.0	9.2	9.1

Source: Government of the Republic of Latvia, Report to the European Union on application for EU Accession, July 1999.
* Source for year 1999 : Central Bureau of Statistics.

The average monthly wage of people employed in the national economy for the first nine months of 1999 compared to the same time in preceding year went up in the average by 7.3% and reached 139.07 lats, an increase from 98.73 lats in 1996, 120.03 lats in 1997 and 133.34 lats in 1998[13]. People employed in education establishments in the public sector, health care and social assistance receive approximately equal level wages – 116 – 117 lats which is still under the average wage of people employed in national economy (by approximately one sixth).[14]

The 1998 Labour Force Survey by the Central Statistics Bureau provides a basic profile of the Latvian labour market:[15]

- In May 1999, Latvia had an economically active population of 1.1601 million, down from 1.177 million in May 1998. These changes reflect a decrease in Latvia's economically active population.

- Between the years 1996 and middle of 1998 there was tendency of growth of the number of the employed. However under the impact of the Russia crisis many enterprise were forced to lay off people. Since May 1999 the number of people employed in national economy has started to rise. The number of people employed increased in 1997, but from May 1998 to the May 1999, the number employed had decreased from 1.007 million to 998 thousand.

- The largest proportions of those employed in May 1999 were in agriculture, hunting and forestry (16.7%), manufacturing (17.4%), and retail and wholesale trade (14.4%). The most significant increase in employment from May 1996 to May 1999 was in retail and wholesale trade (an increase from 12.4% to 14.4%). Employment in education decreased from 10% in 1996 to 8.8% in 1999.

- 50.2% (998 thousand) of the general population older than 15 years of age was employed, but the percentage of employment was higher for those with more education: 72% for those with higher education, approximately 65% for those with secondary professional education, 52% for those with general secondary education, 28% for those with basic education.

- Because of the difficulty of living on a single wage, 5% or 47 thousand of employed work at more than one job.

- The registered unemployment rate started to rapidly grow after August 1998 due to the Russia crisis when it equaled to 7.4% reaching its maximum in April 1999 (10.2%). Since May, unemployment started to go down and in the end of December 1999 it equaled to 9.1% (to compare 9.2% at the end of December 1998). Significant regional disparities continue to present serious problems – in November 1999 the rate was 28.2% in the Rēzekne in the southeastern and historically poorest part of the country, Latgale.[16]

- The share of job seekers in the economically active population varied significantly by education level and gender. The lowest percentage was among those with higher education for both genders, and the highest were among men with less than basic education or basic education, and among both men and women with vocational education. The proportion of job seekers was especially high among women with only vocational education, and secondary general education. Only at levels of secondary professional education (presumably at the higher levels) and higher education did the proportions of job seekers drop significantly. In other words, only for those who complete more than a secondary education does the level of education appear to make a significant difference in obtaining a job.

• Data show significant disadvantages among job seekers for those in rural areas and for women, but the disadvantages for women tend to be most severe for those who have lower levels of education.[17]

The UNDP Latvia Human Development Report 1998 examined the qualitative aspects of the Latvian labour market. The report found significant imbalances in the labour market along several dimensions:

• Long working hours for those who are employed, with limited opportunities to find a job for those who are not.

• Inequalities in access to employment between men and women.

• Significant disparities among regions.

• Major differences between those who speak Latvian and those who do not.

• Disparities between those who are willing and able to move or change careers to obtain a job and those who will not or cannot move or change.

Most relevant to the OECD review was the UNDP finding of a significant mismatch between employers' demand for skilled employees, and the capacity of the education system to produce employees in the professions that are in high demand. The UNDP report emphasises the need for serious structural reforms and for the whole economy to adapt to the rapid process of globalisation. The liberalisation of Latvian trade policies and the recent entrance into the World Trade Organisation will mean that many Latvian enterprises will be unable to compete without fundamental change. These trends portend continuing dramatic changes in the Latvian labour market – and in the expectations regarding the nature and performance of the education system.[18]

Notes

1. Juris Dreifelds. Latvia in Transition. Cambridge: Cambridge University Press, 1996, pp. 4-5.

2. Republic of Latvia, Ministry of Foreign Affairs. "History, Language, Identity and Culture of Latvia," http://www.mfa.gov.lv.

3. Academic Information Centre – Latvian National Observatory. From materials of National report on the modernisation of VET System in Latvia to European Training Foundation, 1999.

4. Academic Information Centre – Latvian National Observatory. From materials of national report on the modernisation of VET System in Latvia to European Training Foundation,1999.

5. Central Statistical Bureau of Latvia. Demographic Yearbook of Latvia, Riga, 1999.

6. United Nations Development Programme. Latvia Human Development Report 1997, p. 37.

7. United Nations Development Programme. Ibid., p. 50.

8. Republic of Latvia, Ministry of Economy. Economic Development of Latvia. Riga: December 1998, pp. 7-10.

9. Central Statistical Bureau uses the International Labour Organisation (ILO) uses a methodology for calculating the unemployment that differs from that used by the State employment service. The ILO definition reveals that the actual percentage of the economically active population (14.5%) that is unemployed is higher than reflected in the SES figure (9.1%).

10. The Human Development Index is calculated on the basis of the average life expectancy, level of education and real GDP per capita determined on the principle of the parity of purchasing power.

11. The Gini Index is a measure of income inequality. The index varies from 0 to 1 and is equal to 0 if there is absolute equality and 1 if there absolute inequality.

12. Republic of Latvia, Ministry of Economy. Economic Development of Latvia. Riga: December 1999, pp. 56.

13. Republic of Latvia, Ministry of Economy. Economic Development of Latvia. Riga: December 1999, p.58.

14. Republic of Latvia, Ministry of Economy. Ibid., p. 58.

15. Republic of Latvia, Ministry of Economy. Ibid., pp. 60-61.

16. Republic of Latvia, Ministry of Economy, Ibid.,p. 60.

17. Academic Information Centre – Latvian National Observatory,. Analysis of the Response of the VET System to the New Economic Objectives in Latvia. Riga: 1998, pp. 20-25. Who Seeks Job in Latvia: Elements of Analysis of the Unemployment Situation in Latvia. Data from the State Statistical Bureau Labour Force Survey and State Employment Service Data on 1997. Riga: 1998.

18. United Nations Development Programme. Latvia Human Development Report 1998. Riga: 1998, pp. 56-72.

Chapter 2

Latvian Education System

Legal framework

The Parliament (*Saeima*) enacts all laws and amendments to laws on education and other laws that affect education as well as the state budget. The Cabinet of Ministers issues all-important education normative acts – regulations. In exceptional cases, the Cabinet of Ministers has the right to issue regulations with the powers of law in between *Saeima* sessions.

The Ministry of Education and Science (MoES) has authority to draft normative acts and draft amendments to normative acts. The MoES has the right to pass binding recommendations to subordinate institutions if the law of regulations prescribe that this institution has the right to choose when taking decisions.

Latvia adopted a Law on Education in 1991. A 1995 Latvian Concept of Education provided the foundation for subsequent changes in the major laws related to education.[1] A new Law on Education enacted in November 1998 serves as the framework for laws related to each of the major education sectors. The Law regulates the education system as a whole and the types and levels of education and educational institutions. It determines the rights and duties of the state, municipal governments, public organisations, professional corporations and associations, private entities, educational institutions, parents, and students. The new Law became effective June 1, 1999.

The Law on Higher Education Establishments was adopted in 1995. Universities have substantial autonomy from the state with respect to establishing and implementing standards and quality assurance, employment policies, and financial affairs. The Council on Higher Education serves as the co-ordinating and quality assurance entity for higher education. The Council's authority is primarily advisory.

43

Figure 6. **Structure of the Ministry of Education and Science of the Republic of Latvia.**

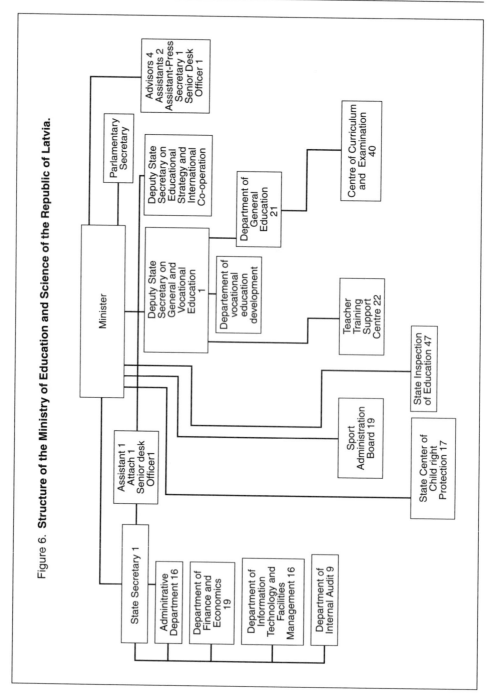

In June 1999, the *Saeima* passed a new Law on General Education and a new Law on Vocational and Professional Education. The MoES has developed a draft law on adult and continuing education.

The MoES has developed a strategic programme for education development, "Education 1998-2003". This programme sets forth strategies for changes at all levels of the education system, including changes in content, structure and financing to be implemented over the four-year period.

Policy structure and governance

Ministry of Education and Science

Within the overall policy structure of the *Saeima* and the Cabinet of Ministers, the MoES is the central executive institution for education in the Republic of Latvia. The organisational structure of the MoES is shown in Figure 6.

Most public pre-schools and schools providing general education at the primary through secondary education levels are the responsibility of municipalities (cities or *pagasts*) subject to oversight by the MoES. The state (national) government pays for teacher salaries and social insurance while the municipalities are responsible for maintenance, capital, and other supporting costs. Local governments (municipalities) from their budget cover the salaries of pedagogical staff of pre-school educational establishments. The state (national) government is directly responsible for most public special schools (*e.g.*, for children with special needs), and most public vocational and secondary professional schools. The state provides most of the funding and the schools are under the authority of the responsibility of the MoES or other ministries (Agriculture, Culture, and Welfare). Higher education institutions have substantial autonomy in governance and financing and public funding comes from the state budget.

In 1998, expenditures from the general government budget for education totalled 246.526 million lats or 15.6% of the total budget. Education expenditures as a percentage of GDP were 6.5% in 1998 with 0.6% earmarked for vocational education and training. These percentages reflect an increase for education overall but a decrease from 1996 regarding vocational education (Figure 7).[2]

Levels and stages of education in Latvia

Education in Latvia uses a modified version of the International Standard Classification of Education (ISCED), with categories as follows (Table 2):

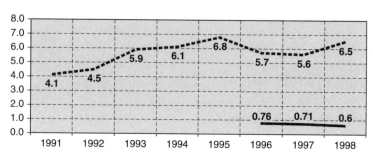

Figure 7. **Education Expenditures as Percentage of GDP.**

`'▪▪▪▪▪` Public expenditure of education as percentage of GDP

`▬▬▬` Public expenditure of VET as percentage of GDP

Source : Academic Information Centre – Latvian National Observatory. From materials of national report on the modernisation of VET System in Latvia to European Training Foundation,1999.

Table 2. **ISCED 97 Levels Compared with Categories Used in Latvia**

ISCED 1997 Levels	Education Categories Adopted in Latvia
0. Pre-primary education	Pre-school education (*pirmsskolas izglītība*).
1. First stage of basic education	Primary education (1-4) (*sākumskola*).
2. Second stage of basic education	Basic secondary education (5-9) (*pamatskola*).
3. Secondary education	General secondary (*vispārejā vidējā izglītība*) Vocational education (*arodizglītība*) Secondary professional education (*vidējā speciālā izglītība*).
4. Postsecondary (non-tertiary) education	The recently enacted (June 1999) Law on Vocational Education and Training formally authorises this level of education, the first level of higher professional education, for the first time in Latvia.
5. First stage of tertiary education	Second level of higher professional education regulated by the Law on Higher Education Establishments.
6. Second stage of tertiary education	Academic higher education professional Higher Education (professional Higher Education based on academic degree).

Figure 8. **Scheme of the Latvian education system.**

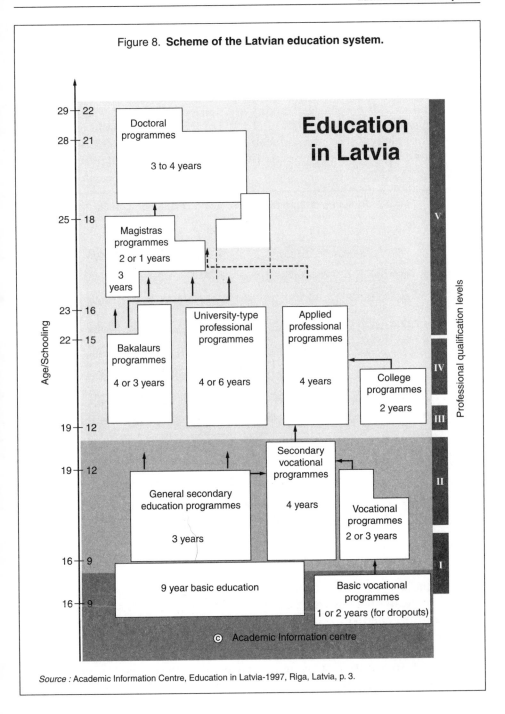

Source : Academic Information Centre, Education in Latvia-1997, Riga, Latvia, p. 3.

Changing structure of enrolments

Figure 9 shows the changing configuration of enrolments in Latvian education institutions over 38 years. The growth in vocational and secondary professional schools in the 1960s and 1970s reflects policies of the Soviet Union during that period, which emphasised highly specialised training of workers for the Soviet economy. Since reaffirmation of Latvian independence, the demand has increased for general secondary education and access to higher education, especially among students who in Soviet times would have entered secondary professional education.

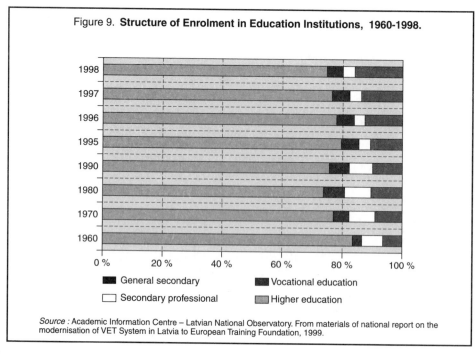

Figure 9. **Structure of Enrolment in Education Institutions, 1960-1998.**

Source : Academic Information Centre – Latvian National Observatory. From materials of national report on the modernisation of VET System in Latvia to European Training Foundation, 1999.

Student flow

In 1999, 32 630 students completed Grade 9 and 31 858 received basic secondary school certificates. Only 772 students (2.4%) completed and did not receive certificates. Of those who obtained certificates, 5% did not continue their education, 20% entered vocational schools, 12% entered secondary professional institutions, and 63% continued into general secondary education.

In 1999, 16 610 students completed general secondary education, and only 209 (1.9%) did not receive certificates. Of these, 60% continued on to higher education, 29% entered the labour market/discontinued their studies, 5% went to vocational schools, and 6% went to secondary professional schools. (Of students graduating from secondary professional education in 1999, 40% went on to higher education, while only 3.8% of vocational secondary students did so.) Figure 10 illustrates these student flows.

Major contextual issues with implications for education policy

In addition to the continuing change of achieving an open, democratic society and sustainable and balanced economic development, Latvia faces four issues that have broad implications for education policy:

- Accession to the European Union.

- Language, ethnicity and social integration.

- Regional disparities and territorial reform.

- Lack of public confidence in government and the need for public administration reform.

The following is a summary of the major developments regarding each of these issues.

Accession to the European Union

The Government of Latvia places high priority on accession to the European Union. Latvia submitted its application for accession in 1995 and adopted a national programme for EU integration in December 1996. In the pre-accession process, Latvia must meet several economic and political conditions demonstrating its ability to assume the conditions of membership. Among the important conditions set forth by the European Council in Copenhagen in June 1993 are that a candidate country has:

- Achieved stability of institutions guaranteeing democracy, the rule of law, human rights and respect for and protection of minorities;

- functioning market economy, as well as the capacity to cope with competitive pressure and market forces within the Union;

- The ability to take on the obligations of membership, including adherence to the aims of political, economic and monetary union. [3]

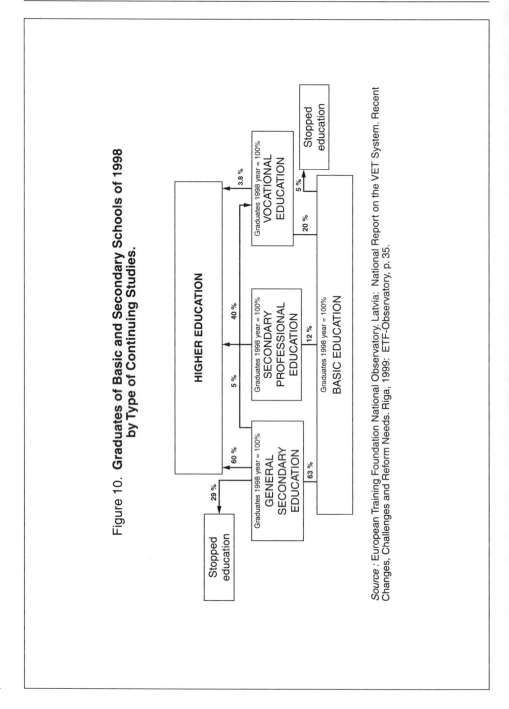

Figure 10. Graduates of Basic and Secondary Schools of 1998 by Type of Continuing Studies.

Source : European Training Foundation National Observatory. Latvia: National Report on the VET System. Recent Changes, Challenges and Reform Needs. Riga, 1999: ETF-Observatory, p. 35.

The European Commission's Progress Report in November 1998 on Latvia's application for EU accession reported that Latvia had taken significant steps in meeting these basic conditions.

The Treaty on European Union (Articles 126 and 127) clearly states that the European Commission fully respects the responsibility of the Member States for the content of teaching and the organisation of education and vocational training systems. The European Commission only supports and supplements the action of Member States. Therefore, preparation for EU accession does not require Latvia to adopt specific EU legislation (formal *acquis communautaire*) other than the urgent need for the strengthening of competitiveness of the Latvian economy and employability of the Latvian workforce. Other requirements for EU accession, such as expectations related to human rights and social integration and sub-national regional structures, have important but indirect implications for education policy.

Language, ethnicity and social integration

In the aftermath of the Soviet period, Latvia faces complex and politically delicate issues related to language, ethnicity, and social integration. In some respects, these issues present the most serious problems for education policy in Latvia. Because they have been addressed extensively in other reports and were being debated actively at the time of the review, the OECD team did not examine these issues in detail, except to observe their pervasive impact on education policy. [4]

- Article 9 of the 1998 Law on Education sets forth requirements that:

- At state and municipal institutions, education shall be acquired in the state language.

- Education may be acquired in another language at a private institution or a state or municipal institution that implements education programmes for national minorities or at other designated institutions.

- Every person must master the state language and take examinations in the state language.

- Examinations for professional qualification must be taken in the state language.

- Papers necessary for qualifying for an academic or scientific degree must be in the state language.

- If increasing a professional qualification or changing a profession is financed from the state or municipal budget, these endeavours must be carried out in the state language.

The 1998 Law on Education, however, provides for gradual implementation of portions of Article 9 that require education to be acquired in Latvian. As of September 1, 1999, the requirements are in effect for institutions of higher education. Institutions with language of instruction other than Latvian must start implementing programmes for national minorities and begin the transition to instruction in Latvian. On September 1, 2004, teaching in Latvian must start in Grade 10 of all state and municipal general institutions, and in the first year of state and municipal vocational institutions.

Increasing the number of institutions in which the language of instruction is Latvian presents a major challenge in developing teachers' Latvian language skills, as well as developing textbooks and teaching materials.

In the June 1999 report on progress toward EU accession, Latvia reported an acceleration of the applications for citizenship following amendments to the law "On Citizenship" following the October 1998 referendum. The government continues to implement the "National Programme for Latvian Language Training" with the assistance of EC Phare and funding from donor countries funding. In December 1998, the second two-year phase of the Programme was started. The progress report also emphasizes that a major development is the adoption of the 1998 Law on Education.

In accordance with the Law, schools with language of instruction other than Latvian will choose either to gradually switch over to Latvian as the language of instruction or to start implementing minority education programmes. The educational establishments will develop these programmes themselves using as the basis the model general education programmes prepared by the Ministry of Education and Science. Four models differ with regard to the proportion of classes to be held in Latvian and minority languages respectively. The schools themselves will choose the model that best suits the interests and language skills of their students. In compliance with the Education Law, the status of educational programmes for minorities has been established and funding of these programmes from the state and municipal budget is guaranteed in general education.[5]

While the proportion of schools in which Latvian is the language of instruction is growing, a significant gap remains between the policy expectations and the realities in the schools. The status of language of instruction is summarised in subsequent sections of this review (pre-school, general education, and vocational and professional education).

Regional disparities and territorial reform

The lack of an effective sub-national governmental structure in Latvia has significant implications for the capacity of Latvia to address serious regional social and economic disparities. As indicated earlier in the review of Latvia's economy, unemployment rates differ significantly among geographic areas. The income differential between rural and urban areas is growing. The Soviet period left Latvia with a distorted regional development, with over concentration of both inhabitants and manufacturing in the Riga region. Industrial enterprises developed in other regions were intended to serve the purposes of the Soviet Union and had no natural connections with a sustainable Latvian economy. The dismantling of large agriculture and industrial enterprises outside the capital exacerbated disparities between Riga and other regions, while few alternative employment opportunities emerged. The gaps are widening, and are particularly worrying in the eastern part of the country, where they are aggravated by low density of population, high unemployment, lower education levels, and an ageing population.

In its first decisions after reaffirmation of independence, Latvia returned to the highly decentralised form of local government that existed before 1940. Rapid decentralisation and democratisation of power characterised the period from 1990 to 1992, reflecting a weak central government and popular distrust of Soviet-era centralised institutions. Substantially increased responsibility was assigned to the smallest unit of government, the *pagast*. As a result of these changes, in the beginning of 1999 there are 483 *pagasts* organised in 26 regions (*rajons*), and 7 metropolitan cities. In the beginning of 1999, almost 40% of *pagasts* had less than 1 000 inhabitants and a further 221 (46%) had between 1 000 and 2 000. Only 10 % of local governments (29 *pagasts* and 28 town cities) had more than 4 000 people. The regions (*rajons*) have limited authority to carry out functions normally associated with sub-national regional governments.[6] In the 1997 opinion on Latvia's application for EU accession, the European Commission commented as follows:

> Latvia manifests a clear political awareness of the need to address rising regional disparities. Given its small size, the decision to maintain regional policy within the framework of the national development strategy seems justified. Clearly, Latvia's needs to improve the administrative structures intended to manage integrated regional development pro-

53

grammes. Yet its administrative capacity should be able to meet these challenges. Thus, subject to the necessary reforms, Latvia should, in the medium-term, be ready to apply Community rules and channel effectively funds from the EC structural policies.[7]

Despite the growing recognition of the need for a functional regional structure between the national and local governments (including requirements of the EU for accession), Latvia has had great difficulty in reaching agreement on such a structure. Meanwhile, significant regional disparities in social and economic problems – and in the capacity of governments to address these problems – continue as major issues facing Latvia.

Territorial reform to establish economically sustainable local authorities is an important element of Latvia's efforts to reduce regional social and economic imbalances. In Fall 1998, the *Saeima* adopted the Law "On Administrative and Territorial Reform." This law proposes a 6-year timeframe for a series of attempts to implement a new regional structure. In the first stage, until December 31, 2003, there would be financial incentives provided to *pagasts* that would volunteer to merge, while in the second stage – from January 1, 2004 until November 30, 2004 – the mergers would be according to projects developed by the national government.

The government has taken several initiatives to address regional development issues and to move toward territorial reform. One of these initiatives is the development of Regional Funds (*Regionu Attistiba-Bezpelnas organizacija valsts sabiedriba ar ierobezotu atbildibu*) to support those regions with low economic and social development resulting from the collapse of the previous economy. The funds available focus on supporting enterprise development by providing education programmes to retrain adults and provide seed money to facilitate access to credit for small enterprise initiatives. A number of regional funds initiatives are administered by different ministries, including the Ministry of Education and Science (MoES).

Nevertheless, at the time of the OECD review in February 1999, there appeared to be no clear and articulated agenda to address disparities in the country. The "Declaration of Work of the Cabinet of Ministers" for the government assuming office in July 1999 states that by 1 January 2001, the Governor "shall ensure significant increase of administrative subdivision scale in order to improve the efficiency of Public Administration."By 1 July 2000, the government intends to "prepare and submit to the *Saeima* the draft law on the establishment of regional municipalities." [8]

The changes in legislation and local government reform have created serious mismatches in authority and responsibility in education. These problems are especially important for pre-school and general education, both of which are local government responsibilities. They also have major implications for regional co-ordination of vocational education and training, and for the capacity of Latvia to meet the expectations on human resource development policy for EU accession.

Lack of public confidence in government and the need for public administration reform

This OECD review focuses primarily on public policy – the actions of the Government of Republic of Latvia and, in particular, the Ministry of Education and Science, to lead education reform. It is important, therefore, as points of context that the Latvian people have low confidence in their governmental institutions and that public administration reform remains one of the major challenges for the Republic. A survey in 1997 of L*atvians' confidence in major institutions found the highest level of confidence in schools, and the lowest confidence in the principal governmental institutions (Table 3).

The survey is also interesting in that although there are differences between citizens and non-citizens, the differences are small when it comes to confidence in government institutions. These consistently low rates for government stem from a range of conditions including attitudes about government developed during the Soviet period. Concerns about governmental corruption are especially important.[9]

Table 3. **Public Confidence in Major Institutions**

The percentage of those who "trusted completely" or "trusted somewhat" major institutions

Institution	Citizens	Non-citizens
Schools	83	70
Local government	52	35
Police	41	47
Cabinet of Ministers	26	22
Saeima	21	22
Political parties	11	10

Source: United Nations Development Programme, Latvian Human Development Report 1998, p.39.

Public administration reform remains one of Latvia's highest priorities. Civil service inherited from Soviet times has an image of red tape and ineffectiveness; reform began in 1992, and the *Saeima* enacted a new Law on State Civil Service in 1994. Actual reform was to take place over two to three years but progress has been slow and the law has been amended repeatedly. The complex process for qualifying to become full civil servants have resulted in large numbers serving only in a "candidate" status, while others have left government and been re-engaged on a contract basis. Low status and low salaries make it difficult for government to compete with the private sector for highly qualified people. As emphasised by the United Nations Development Programme's Latvia Human Development Report 1998, "One of the main tasks of public administration reform in Latvia is the creation of a modern civil service, which would be professional, independent of political parties, and responsible for implementation of state policy."

Frequent changes in government, including six different Prime Ministers since re-establishment of independence, have made sustained attention to public administration reform – and all dimensions of reform – especially difficult. The present government has made the establishment of "economical and efficient public and municipal administration" one of its highest priorities.[11]

As a concluding observation, the team noted a significant reliance on non-governmental organisations (NGOs) and internationally funded projects in the shaping of Latvian education policy and its implementation. This external role is understandable in light of the severe resource constraints within Latvia. While the Ministry of Education and Science developed a Latvian Concept of Education in 1995 that evidently provided a foundation for the subsequent revision of major laws, it is perhaps significant that the no mention of this Concept was made in the course of the OECD review. Consequently, the OECD team sensed that there is much piecemeal change, but little strategic reform in Latvian education. Recurring themes throughout the review mission were fragmentation, lack of coherence, over-specialisation, and lack of accountability throughout the system, in spite of a near-obsession with formulating laws and regulations. "Reform" cannot come from projects or educational innovations alone. Unless it is rooted in the realities of life in Latvia now, and reaches toward a shared vision for Latvia's future, reform will remain at best a legal abstraction, and at worst an unwanted irritation to schools struggling to survive. It is a shared, national vision that is needed; its absence hampers strategic thinking, planning and policy leadership. Its formation would bring much-needed coherence to the reform effort; it might also strengthen public confidence in government, and support national unity as Latvia prepares for EU accession.

Notes

1. Republic of Latvia, Ministry of Education and Science, Latvian Concept of Education, Riga: 1998.

2. Data for 1998 obtained from draft ETF report on the status of Latvian vocational education and training in relationship to the *acquis communautaire*, September 1999 (Hanna Autere).

3. European Commission, Agenda 2000: Commission Opinion on Latvia's Application for Membership of the European Union, June 1997.

4. See Republic of Latvia. Human Rights and Social Integration in the Republic of Latvia: A General Survey. National Report of Latvia Ministry of Foreign Affairs and Nationalisation Board for the United Nations Development Programme Regional Meeting in Yalta 22-4 September 1998 – "Human Rights for Human Development." Republic of Latvia, "Latvia's Contribution to the Report from the Commission on Latvia's Progress Toward Accession (National Progress Report), Riga, June 1999, United Nations Development Programme, "National Integration and Social Cohesion," Latvia: Human Development Report. Riga: 1997, pp. 48-66.

5. Republic of Latvia. "Latvia's Contribution to the Report from the Commission on Latvia's Progress Toward Accession" (National Progress Report). Riga: June 1999, p. 10.

6. United Nations Development Programme. "Regional Development". Latvia: Human Development Report. Riga: 1997, pp. 67-82.

7. European Commission, Agenda 2000: Commission Opinion on Latvia's Application for Membership of the European Union, June 1997.

8. Republic of Latvia, Cabinet of Ministers. "Declaration on the Work of the Cabinet of Ministers". Riga: July 1999.

9. United Nations Development Programme. Latvia Human Development Report 1998. Riga: pp. 38-40.

10. United Nations Development Programme. Ibid., p. 50.

11. Republic of Latvia, Cabinet of Ministers, "Declaration on the Work of the Cabinet of Ministers". Riga: July 1999.

Chapter 3

Compulsory and General Education

Policy structure and national governance

The Law on Education (Article 4) as adopted in October 1998 specified that compulsory (mandatory) education includes "preparation of children of age five and six for primary education, and primary education or the continuing of primary education until reaching age 18". Latvia, therefore, was committed to beginning compulsory education at the level of pre-school. In amendments to the 1998 Law on Education adopted on 5 August 1999, however, the reference to "preparation of children age five and six for primary education was eliminated. Therefore, compulsory education in Latvia now begins with primarily education and extends through primary or basic nine-year education. If a student does not or is unable to complete primary education, he or she is still covered by the mandatory requirements until age 18.

As described in the preceding chapter, the Ministry of Education and Science (MoES) is the central executive institution for education in Latvia, under the overall direction of Parliament and the Cabinet of Ministers and within the framework of Latvia's Constitution and laws. The MoES has responsibility for schools and institutions under its direct supervision, including vocational schools, schools for special populations, and programmes for national minorities. However, pre-school, primary, and general secondary education schools are under the governing authority of local municipalities. The MoES, therefore, has responsibility for drawing up national standards, and other regulatory, oversight, quality assurance, and technical assistance/support func-tions with respect to these schools, but the MoES has a more direct supervisory role in other sectors.

Local and regional governance

Municipalities

Every municipality, including the 483 *pagasts* and the seven metropolitan cities, is obliged to provide children residing in its territory with the possibility to acquire pre-school and primary education at an educational institution which is closest to the place of residence. Municipalities are also obliged to provide youth with the opportunity to acquire secondary education. The law provides students with the freedom to choose a school in another municipality to be financed through contracts between municipalities.

In addition to its education responsibilities, the local government of the *pagast* is responsible for the full range of municipal functions (*e.g.*, maintaining roads) as defined by the Law on Local Governments. Citizens elect a *pagast* council which serves as the policy-making entity for the municipality.

Among their specific education responsibilities, municipalities shall:

- In co-ordination with the MoES, establish, re-organise and close pre-schools, primary and elementary and secondary schools.

- Provide children who have reached compulsory school age and who reside in its administrative territory with places in pre-schools, primary schools and secondary general schools.

- In co-ordination with the MoES employ and dismiss heads of institutions under their supervision.

- Establish the procedure for the financing of educational institutions under their supervision from the municipality budgets; in accordance with mutual agreements, participate in the financing of state educational institutions, educational institutions of other municipalities and private educational institutions; distribute and allocate the financial means from the municipality budgets to educational institutions and control the rationality of expenditure.

- Maintain the facilities of the schools under its supervision ensuring that their financing is no less than the minimum levels established by the Cabinet of Ministers.

- Guarantee the transfer of funds allotted from the state budget for teachers' salaries and state subsidies into the accounts of schools.

- Provide financing for the technical staff (maintenance, security, and other non-instructional staff).

- Provide students with preventive and first aid medical care; and

- Provide heat, electricity, and other utilities for the schools.

Under the authority of the *pagast*, school principals are responsible for daily operation of their schools, including hiring and dismissing teachers, setting salaries within the required state minimum levels. The principals also have the authority to – and usually must – generate additional non-state resources for the school by reaching out to sponsors, parents, and donors.

Boards of education

In the seven metropolitan cities, Boards of Education (school boards) are at the level of the city municipality and integrated with the municipal education administration. In other areas of Latvia, the school boards function at the regional municipal level. As discussed earlier in this OECD review, regional entities in Latvia are only at a developmental stage and currently have limited authority in relation to the *pagasts*. In the case of regional municipal school boards, these entities function within the authority of regional councils composed of the chairmen of the elected councils of each of the *pagasts* within the region. By law, the heads of school boards must be professional educators. Regional municipal school boards can have direct supervisory responsibility for some schools (*e.g.*, boarding schools, vocational schools, or specialised schools for students with special needs). The regional municipal boards' principal functions related to schools under the authority of *pagasts* are to provide technical assistance and support for schools. The formal responsibilities defined in the Law on Education are limited, but the MoES has been delegating to these regional entities the responsibility for a wider range of functions such as in-service education and instructional support for individual schools. Among their responsibilities, school boards:

- Undertake efforts to improve the qualifications of teachers within the regions.

- Co-ordinate and provide methodological support.

- Organise education for adults.

- Assist schools by providing teaching and methodological materials.

The most important function of regional school boards is to implement the region council's or district council's education policy and allocate funds from the state (national) budget to the schools within the region, for teachers' salaries and social insurance.

Financing

Both the state and municipalities provide financing for pre-school, primary (basic) education and general secondary education. The state directly supervises and provides funding for vocational and secondary professional schools, special schools, programmes for national education, special education, and "social corrective" education. Basically, the division of responsibility between the state (national government) and municipalities is as follows:

- The state finances the salaries and social insurance costs of teachers according to policies and norms established by the Cabinet of Ministers. The state also provides funding for textbooks. These funds are budgeted as a line item in the MoES budget and allocated to school boards based on norms per student. Funding is also reserved in the salary fund (approximately 2%) for accredited private schools.

- Municipalities (*pagasts* and metropolitan cities) provide financing for learning materials, maintenance and repair of school buildings, technical (non-instructional) school personnel (*e.g.*, cleaning, maintenance and security), student meals, and utilities (heating and electricity). The Cabinet of Ministers establishes certain minimum levels of funding to ensure a degree of consistency of provision across the country.

Teacher salaries and school funding

Latvia agreed to reforms in school financing in 1996 and these are still in the process of being implemented. The new policy is designed on the principle of norm-based per-student funding. An important feature of the 1996 reforms is that the funds for teachers' pay are not allocated directly from the state to individual municipalities (except in the case of metropolitan cities), but are allocated as a lump sum to the regional school boards.

The target allocation to each regional school board is based on a minimum wage established by the Cabinet of Ministers per teaching position. The number of teaching positions in each region (and therefore the amount of the lump sum target allocation to the region) is a calculated figure, and is not based on the actual number of teachers. The target allocation for teachers' salaries is allocated to the region's school board on the basis of normed number of students in the region. The number of teachers is calculated on the basis of one teacher per 21 students, multiplied by coefficients reflecting the number of hours and complexity of the study plans at each level, regional characteristics (urban/rural) and other variables.

The schools develop budgets for each new school year, taking into consideration teacher study plans (reflected in content and hours), minimum and maximum class sizes, and other variables. The regional school boards are responsible for reconciling the difference between the total teacher salary bill projected for schools within the region, and the state's target allocations.

Consequently, the school board has authority – at least in theory – to reallocate funds among schools and to provide incentives for optimisation such as developing larger secondary schools to serve students from more than one *pagast*. In the severe economic conditions facing Latvia as a whole and individual regions and *pagasts* in particular, significant differences exist between plans and actual funding. Regions do not receive the full state fund for target allocations, and schools receive less than their proposed budgets. Teachers carry out on average 1.3 teaching positions. The formula generating the regional target allocations would have caused reallocation among regions, but hold-harmless agreements blunted the potential impact of these changes.

Therefore, despite progress toward a more equitable and efficient funding system for schools, Latvia continues to face severe disparities among regions. Wealthier municipalities (Riga, Ventspils, and other metropolitan cities) are able to provide substantial supplements to state-funded teacher salaries, while others are unable to provide these supplements or, for that manner, to meet the state-mandated minimum municipal funding requirements for maintenance of facilities.

Municipal (pagast) financing of schools

Municipalities, as set out above, provide a substantial part of school finance. Because of the extreme variation in size and fiscal capacity of *pagasts* across the country, Latvia has enacted public finance reforms that give some consideration to equity. Centrally collected revenues from taxes on personal and business income, imports, retail sales and specific goods are now shared with municipalities according to a pre-established formula. All revenues from personal income tax are returned to the local municipality in which the taxpayer resides. However, the state retains all other centrally collected revenues, and some of these are used to fund a system of categorical transfers to municipalities and a revenue equalisation fund. The categorical transfers are intended to provide sufficient funds to allow local governments to fulfil nationally mandated minimum service standards for education, health care and social protection. The equalisation fund permits all local governments to provide minimum levels of local amenities such as street lighting and maintenance of public parks.

63

The equalisation fund closes 70% of the gap between actual per-capita reve-nue and national averages. Neither of these two transfers is earmarked for edu-cation. Consequently, the needs of schools must compete with other local needs for funding. For example, the cost of school heating and electricity can consume more than half the budget of some small *pagasts*, but savings in school utility costs would not necessary return to the schools, and could be used to meet other demands on the *pagast's* budget.

Kinds of institutions

The Context chapter of this review sets out the basic structure of the Latvian education system (see especially Figure 9 showing students' progression from pre-school through higher education). Compulsory education starts at age five or six, and the Law on Education specifies an obligation to "acquire primary (basic, nine-year) education"; this obligation remains until the age of 18.[1]

In the 1998 Law on Education, one year of pre-school (*pirmsskola*) was esta-blished as the first stage of mandatory (*compulsory*) education in Latvia for five or six-year olds. Comparable to kindergarten in other countries, "pre-school" was established more clearly as an educational institution, in contrast to its earlier, primarily social and custodial role. As mentioned above, amendments to the Law on Education adopted in August 1999, eliminated pre-school as the first stage of compulsory education. The decision to eliminate this provision was apparently made primarily for financial reasons. The OECD team recognises the major implications for financing and for teacher preparation and retraining of extending compulsory education to the pre-school level. Nevertheless, effec-tive pre-school education is one of the most important means for a country to improve the lives and subsequent learning of young children. At the time of the visit to Latvia, the OECD team viewed the Latvia's commitment to making pre-school the initial stage of compulsory education as a positive development. The team considers it as an unfortunate – and hopefully only short-term – deve-lopment that Latvia decided withdraw that commitment through the August 1999 amendment.

Basic education (*pamatizglītība*) is the second stage of compulsory education. It begins at age six or seven, and lasts a total of nine years – four years of primary (*sākumskola*) followed by five years of lower secondary school (*pamatskola*). Graduates receive a certificate of basic (nine-year) school completion (*atestāts par pamatizglītību*). The end of *pamatskola* marks the end of compulsory schooling, although students who have not completed the requirements must continue until they finish the programme or until they reach the age of 18.[1]

After leaving *pamatskola*, students have a range of options for further, non-compulsory schooling. Professional (*vidēja speciālā izglītība*) and vocational (*arodizglītība*) secondary education are discussed in a separate chapter in this review. General secondary education (*vispārējā vidizglītība*), falls under the governing authority of local municipalities. To be awarded a certificate of general secondary education (*atestāts par vispārēja vidēja izglītību*) students have to pass final examinations in core and reach a satisfactory level in seven non-examination subjects. All holders of this atestats are eligible for admission to higher education. Curriculum and assessment issues are discussed later in this chapter.

Numbers of schools, enrolments, language of instruction

Pre-school establishments (Pirmsskolas iestazu)

Between 1995/96 and 1998/99, the number of pre-school establishments decreased from 608 to 586 or by 3.6%. During the same period the number of students decreased from 72 847 to 66 143 (9.5%) and instructional staff decreased from 9 015 to 8 547 (6%). At the same time the number of privately owned establishments increased from three to ten and private school enrolments increased from 156 to 278.[2]

Declining birth rate and compulsory pre-school for 5-6 year olds

These two issues appear unrelated, but both affect "school life", especially in primary schools. Latvia's school-age population is shrinking rapidly: between 1990 and 1998, the number of children born annually fell by 52% – from 37 918 in 1990 to 18 410 in 1998. By 1996, the total fertility rate for Latvian women had fallen to 1.16, the lowest any nation has ever reported.[3] School enrolments have

Table 4. **Pre-school enrolments**

Year	Latvian		Russian		Polish		Latvian and Russian		Other	
	Enrol-ment	%	Enrol-ment	%	Enrol-t ment	%	Enrol-ment	%	Enrol ment	%
1995/96	48 066	66.0	24 466	33.6	232	0.3	57	0.1	26	0.04
1998/99	47 015	71.1	16 688	25.2	186	0.3	2 254	3.4	--	

Source: MoES, Education in Latvia, 1995/96 to 1998/99, p. 9.

begun to show the effects, and first-year enrolments will continue to decline at least until 2003 when they will reach less than half (46%) of their 1998 level (Table 4). An appropriate policy response to this decline is not yet clear, but with fewer children arriving at the school door, it will become even harder for the education sector to justify maintaining small schools and very low (by international standards) student:teacher ratios – only 9.9 students for each teacher nationally, and teachers working on average only 17.9 hours per week In 1990, nearly 75% of the 0-6 age group was in school; by 1998, it was only about 40.3%. There is thus a genuine educational concern that more youngsters arrive at "Big School" completely unprepared. At the time of the OECD review, the 1998 Law on Education extended compulsory education to the 5-6 year age group and aligned school starting age with European practice. This provision was eliminated through August 1999 amendments to the Law on Education. The OECD team observed that compulsory pre-school education would help with early diagnostics of learning problems, and give non-Latvian speaking children an extra year to catch up. Realistically, however, it would also be a way for schools to retain staff despite falling enrolments.

Implementation of compulsory pre-school education as originally envisioned in the 1998 Law on Education clearly represented a major challenge for Latvia. The team heard that some municipalities would have significant problems accommodating the full 5-6 year cohort, but that most would be able to cope. There were a new set of educational standards for pre-schools, emphasising child development rather than reading, writing and numbers. At the time of the review, the team observed that, on the whole, extending compulsory schooling to all 5-6 year olds is a sensible move – as long as poorer municipalities receive some extra support. It is therefore of concern that the August 1999 amendment eliminated this provision.

Comprehensive schools [4]

Between 1995/96 and 1998/99, the number of comprehensive schools, both full-time and part-time, stabilised at 1 111, including 1 074 full-time schools (Table 5) and 37 part-time schools. In the beginning of school year 1999/00 due to optimisation of school network the number of schools decreases to 1095. The number of private schools increased from 24 in 1995/96 to 48 in 1999/00, primarily at the secondary level. At the same time, comprehensive school enrolments (full and part-time) increased from 347 541 to 361 432, or 3.8%. There were major differences by level. In Grades 7 through 9, enrolments decreased from 95 452 to 88 029 or by 7.8% between 1995/96 and 1999/00. However, reflecting the increased demand for general secondary education (often as a potential pathway to higher education), enrolments in Grades 10 through 12 increased by 32.4% or from 37 472 to 49 643. Part-time and private school enrolments, although they are only a small proportion of overall enrolments, increased the fastest, especially in Grades 10 to 12. From 1995/96 to 1999/00, part-time enrolment increased from 9 881 to 14380 (45%) and private school enrolments from 1 655 to 3 007 (82%).[5]

The proportion of children whose language of instruction is Latvian increased from 61.6% in 1995/96 to 66.3% in 1998/99.[6] The previous year, 1997/98, the language of instruction was Latvian in 69% of the comprehensive schools and for 57% of the students (Table 6). In Riga – reflecting regional differences in population concentration – Latvian was the only language of instruction in only 51% of the schools and for 39% of the enrolments. In rural areas, except in the southeast, the percentages of children whose language of instruction is Latvian were significantly higher than in Riga and other cities.[7]

There were 35 880 instructional staff, including multiple job-holders, for an enrolment of 361 722 students in comprehensive schools 1998/99. Most of these instructional staff (97%) and students (96%) were in comprehensive full-time schools.[8]

Table 5. **Comprehensive[1] full-time schools**
Beginning of School Year 1997/98

Number of schools		Primary		Basic		Secondary		Special	
Total	Rural	Total	Rural	Total	Rural	Total	Rural	Total	Rural
1 074	637	105	62	533	434	384	107	56	34
Enrolment									
Total	Rural								
348 205	98 788	11 746	2 456	89 296	56 301	238 800	36 170	8363	3 861
Students per school									
323.3	155.1	113.9	39.6	167.8	129.7	625.1	338.0	147.9	113.6

1. MoES, *Education in Latvia, 1995/96 to 1998/99*, Riga: 1999.
Source: Republic of Latvia, Central Statistical Bureau, Education Institutions in Latvia and the Beginning of School Year 1997/98, pp. 30-59.

Table 6. **Comprehensive[1] Schools by Language of Instruction**
1996/97 – 1998/99

	1996/97		1998/99		1996/97		1998/99	
	Schools		Schools		Enrolment		Enrolment	
	number	%	number	%	number	%	number	%
Total	1 019		1 018		334 646		339 842	
Latvian	682	67	699	69	181 297	54.2	194 342	57.1
Russian	194	19	185	18	110 886	33.1	103 953	30.7
Latvian and Russian	137	13.4	128	12.6	25 805	12.45	26 236	11.9
					15 750		14 138	
Polish	5	0.5		0.5	656	0.2	846	0.24
Ukrainian	1	0.1	1	0.1	185	0.05	251	0.06

1. *school in Riga with grades providing tuition in Belarussian (47 pupils); 1 school in Liepaja with grades providing tuition in Lithuanian (29 pupils)*

Source: Republic of Latvia, Central Statistical Bureau, Education Institutions in Latvia at the Beginning of School Year 1998/99, pp. 40-43.

Issues

In the course of the review, the OECD team identified a number of promising developments in Latvia's education reform as well as issues of concern when Latvia's reforms are placed in a comparative perspective. The following is an overview of several of those developments and issues.

Quality

The quality of an education system has three main building blocks: the quality of input (education funding, buildings, staff, textbooks and materials); the quality of process (curriculum, teaching quality, class sizes, time spent in school); and the quality of "output", or student achievement. All three are necessary for educational quality, but the first two are important only insofar as they contribute to the last – to student learning.

Quality monitoring system

In Latvia, some mechanisms are being put in place. Changes are being made in administration and finance flows to ensure greater local control. Other changes include wider choice in textbooks and materials, curriculum revision and reform, and new approaches to teacher evaluation and in-service training.

What is still lacking is an overall framework for quality control, whereby the Minister receives regular, reliable information about educational quality that can be used for legal and policy change. The team is concerned that greater local control, while desirable in itself, also deprives the Ministry of effective means to hold local authorities accountable for the quality of education they provide. Decentralisation without accountability is a double-edged sword.

The proposed World Bank/Government of Latvia Education Improvement Project[9] emphasises the development of such an overall quality framework The Project was not yet in operation at the time of the OECD review, but it is encouraging that the Latvian Government sees quality improvement as a priority.

Several reasons can be identified for this new focus. First, in Soviet times the inputs and processes of education were minutely controlled, so it was assumed that outcomes were predictable and did not need to be closely checked or internationally compared. Now, as controls loosen and educational provision diversifies, policy makers need to establish nationally reliable ways to monitor quality – especially output quality – not only in national but also in European terms. Second, school tests and leaving examinations were not the real gatekeepers to desirable university places or jobs – these were allocated on a different basis altogether, and therefore school assessment was generally low-stakes and low-priority. It was also cheap. Ministries of Education did not spend money on assessment; few had any permanent staff assigned to it at all. In Latvia, teachers had until recently the responsibility and the freedom to set and mark school leaving examinations for their own students. The need now is for a more objective, transparent, nationally comparable assessment system. The national curriculum and examinations centre (*Izglitibas Satura un Eksaminacijas Centrs* or ISEC) within the Ministry is gradually introducing centrally marked examinations, but the centre is still new, small in size and financial resources, and limited in the number of subjects it is able to examine.

Third, the post-1991 enthusiasm for decentralisation brought with it a countervailing, perhaps paradoxical, need to set up central control mechanisms. These central mechanisms are necessary to safeguard a unified, national vision of Latvian education, and protect every child's right to education of essentially the same quality, regardless of who or where the child may be. Now that *rajons*, municipalities and schools have more control – and the Ministry has neither the money nor the authority to investigate what goes on – it is no longer possible to know what quality is delivered in the classroom.

Since 1991, inspectorates in many former Soviet Union countries have lost their legitimate mandate along with their much-resented role as political enforcers. Although in Latvia there is still a Ministry-based Inspectorate, the team heard that school inspectors do not monitor teaching and learning. They check documents, ensure that school registers are correctly kept, and that the school complies with basic requirements such as heating, time-tabling, etc. Each inspector is responsible for about 40 schools; transport can be a problem; a school visit lasts no more than half a day or a day, not giving enough time to understand the school or form an accurate impression of its educational quality. Methodologists (subject advisers) exist in all *rajons*, but they, too, are severely stretched and not always able to travel to schools to support classroom teachers. Because of low compensation levels and extensive workloads, it is difficult to attract and retain qualified methodologists.

Latvia needs a new system for the regular evaluation of school quality. The proposed self-assessment and accreditation process will go a long way towards this, but school improvement is an intensive, long-term team effort requiring much more than paperwork. A revitalised professional inspectorate would be a key channel to bring reforms into schools and classrooms, and to provide essential support to teachers.

Standards

Two major trends are apparent in OECD countries as well as in the new democracies in Eastern and Central Europe and former Soviet Union: the search for educational standards to ensure the quality of education; and a shift from the acquisition of knowledge to its application to real-life problems. Both are based on the idea that educational quality depends on how a student's mind is formed, not how it is filled.

Educators in Latvia are well aware that much teaching and learning in schools and universities now is knowledge-based rather than aimed at analytical and critical thinking skills and practical application. Of course, progress in learning does require a sound basis of essential literacy and numeracy skills, and a sufficient level of factual knowledge; but it should not stop there. Modern life demands young people who can evaluate what they see in the world around them and act responsibly and creatively on what they see. Modern education, then, should aim to produce young people capable of acting for themselves, of making reasonable judgements based on intelligently assessed evidence. Reason, judgement, action, and imagination are needed, as well as factual knowledge.

Subject standards (in effect, curriculum content requirements) were introduced in Latvia in 1992 but remained little more than a list of knowledge to be covered and assessed at each Grade. In 1996, the MoES began a two-year process of developing the National Compulsory Education Standard, which sets out reforms to be achieved by the year 2005. This is much more than mere curriculum reform for compulsory schooling (Grades 1-9). It means to accomplish fundamental educational reform, guided by three principles:

- A change in focus, from the acquisition of knowledge to its application and use;

- A practical orientation, emphasising problem solving and active skills;

- Better linkages and integration among curriculum subjects, to avoid gaps and overload.

The National Standards of Compulsory Education (Grades 1-9) were developed over two years, with some outside consultation and much publicity. Parents were not closely involved. Not many parents expressed an interest in participating, although opportunities for comment did exist.

The new Standards were approved in April 1998 and are contained in what is known as the "Yellow Book" now available in all basic schools in Latvia. It emphasises modern-day Latvian values such as unity – including a transition to Latvian as the "language of national unification"; universality and equality for all including those with special needs; integration of the education system; and schooling as a basis for life-long learning.[10]

The main objective of the National Standards is to provide a framework within which *rajons* and schools can design localised syllabi, modifying content as necessary without losing the Standards' requirements. The structure is that of a table setting out the components of compulsory education (mathematical skills, communicative skills, social skills, moral and aesthetic skills) along one axis. Along the other axis are the "educational spheres" (Language, Self & Society, The Arts, and Natural Sciences). The result is a complex, colour-coded grid. Traditional subjects are fitted into this larger conceptual framework, showing criss-crossing linkages between sports and Self & Society; Arts and history, etc.[11]

The "Yellow Book" is a remarkable achievement. The team found it was widely accepted by school heads and teachers. However, the team also heard some criticism of the complexity of the new curriculum structure, and a great deal of uncertainty about its implementation in the classroom.

Dissenting views on the National Standards

There is still a wide gap between the expectations of the new Standards and classroom practice. The team was told, "Teachers have four resources: the textbook, the timetable with some new flexibility built in, the content standards set in 1995, and the 'Yellow Book'. There is a gap between standards and testing: that gap is the "black box of teaching". Teachers say they need subject standards and study programmes to support the Standards "roof"; they also want their four basic resources to be mutually compatible instead of at odds with each other.

Teachers also say that the textbooks they have are based on the old standards; and unless a new generation of textbooks can be provided along with the new Standards, there is a risk that teaching and learning will remain knowledge-based and subject-bound, as they are at present. Furthermore, opinions vary about the nature of the Standards: some see them more as overall goals towards which schools should work, while others interpret them as strict requirements.

.   Some concepts inherent in the new Standards – such as the distinction between proficiency and achievement in student learning – are not clear to teachers. The team heard that the new-style exams are more easily accepted by students than by their teachers, who find it difficult to adjust their teaching styles and consider some of the new tests too demanding. Nor do all teachers have the creativity and independence to make optimal use of the new flexibility provided by optional subjects and Project Weeks, or to adapt their knowledge-based materials to a more active, competence-based approach.

Standards: the way forward

It is clear to the team that teachers will need substantial support and in-service training to deal with these innovations. The basic message is: the greater the flexibility and complexity, the greater the demands on teacher competence, teacher involvement at the school level, and school culture.

Several OECD countries have developed their curricula in directions similar to those observed in Latvia today. Experience shows that the more diverse and complex the process of learning and its expected outcomes are, the more difficult it is to set detailed, externally predetermined programmes for teaching. In other words, when the intended outcomes of student learning go beyond mastering knowledge and related basic skills, centrally planned teaching becomes more difficult. In light of experiences elsewhere, Latvia – like any other country where the outcomes of education are expected to respond to the needs of the new societies – needs to strengthen the active planning of teaching at the school level. Teachers should not only decide upon the way they teach given topics, but also clarify and conceptualise the ultimate purpose and aims of teaching, so that they can identify clear linkages between their subjects and the entire mission of their schools.

Thus far, the National Standards cover only the compulsory schooling period up to the end of Grade 9. It will be important to ensure that similar standards are developed for upper secondary schooling, including general (*vispārējā vidējā izglītība*), vocational (*arodizglītība*), and professional (*vidēja speciālā izglītība*) secondary education. Agreed national standards here are particularly important, because these sectors lead to employment qualifications or to entrance into higher education. The standards therefore need to take into account the expectations of employers and universities while still maintaining the principles of unity and access for all. It will be essential to involve representatives from the higher education sector and from employers (as well as professional educators and Ministry officials) in their development. The OECD team was informed that these points are stipulated in the Law on Vocational Education and are being taken into consideration in the development of general secondary education standards.

Standards are also needed for schools under the jurisdiction of other Ministries – for example, the Ministry of Culture or the Ministry of Agriculture. It will be important to ensure that those standards, at least for core subjects, do not differ substantially from those set by the MoES; it might be useful to have MoES representation on standards working groups in other sectors.

Curriculum and teaching

Teaching and learning in the classroom

Writers on post-1989 developments tend to see education reform in terms of large issues like finance, standards, curriculum reform, teacher training, links between school and employment, and so on. These seem to lend themselves most readily to legal and policy solutions: areas where we can "do something" that will be visible over the span of, for example, a five-year project.

However, the real work of schools happens in classrooms. The ways in which children's lives are affected there are hard to measure but are likely to be more important than whether a particular slice of the curriculum is taught in some new, attractive way. At present in Latvia, many schools are more concerned with survival than with change. So are many communities, families, and children. It could even be said that the unchanging classroom has become a symbol of comfort and stability. The women presiding over these classrooms, weary of reform without resources, do not see their first duty to innovation but to the safe-keeping of children and of old-fashioned values like discipline and the unchanging "certainty" of textbook and timetable in a sea of unpredictable change.

The challenge now is to adopt what is new without losing or downgrading what is good in Latvian classrooms. Teachers should understand that sustainable change occurs by starting where they are today and then assessing carefully where changes are needed. Dedication to the arts, languages and sports should continue to be vital elements of teaching and curriculum in schools. New ideas should emerge through the existing strengths and not from external initiatives alone.

Knowledge, skills and attitudes for new conditions

The legacy of the Soviet era can still be observed in Latvian schools: teachers tend to deliver externally designed study programmes, with little adjustment of content or aims to the specific situation of their students. Yet Latvia's transition from a command economy to a free market economy calls for different skills and attitudes that are essential both for the labour force and for the consumers of its products.

From the pedagogical perspective, this means that in teaching and learning the non-cognitive areas of human development should have equal status with the traditional acquisition of knowledge. Problem-solving, co-operation with others, and self-reliance are life skills that should be practised and valued in the classroom. The Standards contained in the "Yellow Book" (see above, MoES 1998) emphasise the development of thinking skills, co-operative working methods, and greater scope for creativity among teachers in schools. The review team was also encouraged to find several contemporary research and development projects in teacher training institutions and their collaborating schools; however, the road from ideas and intentions to classroom practice is always longer and harder than expected.

The meaning of "curriculum"

One obstacle to modern curriculum development in Latvia is a lack of consensus on what curriculum means. More precisely, the Latvian language does not have a term that corresponds to the modern concept of "curriculum". The team found that in most contexts, curriculum is understood as "programmes of study", "syllabuses", or simply teaching plans with numbers of hours allocated for each school subject. In its conversations with education experts, teachers, and researchers during the OECD mission, the team noted considerable confusion when "curriculum" was understood in different ways. This is not merely a matter of semantics: there is a conceptual issue at stake as well.

The whole notion of curriculum development is devalued if it is limited to matters of content, sequences, and other technical aspects rather than focusing on ways to organise teaching to promote students' interests and good learning. It will be also difficult to link the Latvian school improvement effort with international trends if inconsistent terms are used. The concept of curriculum development has a wide international currency among educators; when this term is missing or loosely defined, there will be major problems in connecting the thinking of Latvian experts to that of their international partners. Emphasis on learning and the context of teaching will remain weak, with a focus on content and sequencing rather than on designing learning environments that promote students' curiosity. Most seriously of all, curriculum development will remain at best the domain of specialised teams in school, rather than a dynamic whole-school activity.

The present situation

In the Latvian context, instead of curriculum development there is a curriculum system consisting of four basic elements, all regulated from "above": general national standards, specific subject standards (not yet available for all subjects), programmes of study, and the common time-table. National standards are now ready for pre-school and compulsory education in Grades 1 to 9. National standards for general secondary education are under preparation. These documents, as part of a curriculum "system", provide the overall aims of schooling and of each subject together with a description of content and time allocations. This, indeed, is how many countries regulate and steer their teachers' work. In Latvia, however, the system appears to be almost exclusively top-down, providing little relevant involvement of classroom teachers in the actual planning of teaching and learning.

To supplement these official documents, each school prepares a school development plan and a work plan. The school development plan is a longer-term strategic paper that describes the school's aims, and sets out the means by which the school plans to organise its work in order to achieve them The annual work plan, in turn, contains the time allocation for each subject, a plan for using school space, and possible themes and special days during the next academic year. In most schools, specific teams of teachers and assistant heads are in charge of preparing these documents.

75

All standards have to be approved by the MoES, while programmes of study (courses) may be authorised at school level. (Schools are free to propose new standards to the Ministry in those subjects where there are no national standards, such as the Finnish language.) The teachers themselves develop the respective programmes of study, and the school principal then approves these.

Although recent (1999/00 school year) transfer to the schools more responsibility for the design and selection of programmes and profiles, the sample lesson plans adopted by the MoES in 1998 remain a source of guidance for general education and for evening and correspondence schools. Each school is also still mandated to ensure that syllabuses must be in accordance with educational standards, the interests of students, and the character of the school and its teachers.

In elementary (*sakumskola*, Grades 1-4) and primary (*pamatskola*, Grades 5-9), the subjects |but not necessarily the exact content covered by the sample lesson plans are compulsory. In *sakumskola*, for example, students are taught Latvian, English and one other foreign language, mathematics, natural sciences, music, arts, handicrafts, and physical education. The weekly number of lessons rises from 20 to 24 during the course of this cycle. There are two to three optional lessons in each Grade for all students. In addition, there is some variance in the number of some school subjects, based on the possibilities and characteristics of each school. The document specifies a separate time allocation for schools of non-Latvian language tuition where foreign languages are replaced by the students' own language.

The sample lesson plans for *pamatskola* (Grades 5-9) share similar characteristics with those for the lower Grades. There is flexibility in the number of lessons for most subjects, together with four totally optional lessons each year. Similarly, non-Latvian language schools have their own lesson plans with minor variations to those of Latvian language schools.

The lesson plans for general secondary schools (*vispareja videja izglitiba*) have two sections: one outlining compulsory subjects, and the other optional ones. Both sections have varying numbers of basic (*pamat*) and profile (*profil*) courses. Each subject is graded according to the total number of hours a in three-year period, and points are given accordingly. All students must study each of the optional courses at either *pamat* or *profil* level. From the list of optional courses offered by their specific school, students can select their courses so that the total number of the points indicating the students' study load lies between 90 and 180 points, or the total number of lessons within the three years is between 3 150 and 3 780 lessons. There are at least five compulsory examinations at the end. The minimum size of examinable courses is 105 lessons.

The recent (1999/00) changes mean that schools have greater freedom in designing programmes and profiles. A school may introduce subjects or integrated themes that are not included in state lesson plans, standards, or programmes; it can build its own individual profile by emphasising some subjects (such as languages and literature) and giving less attention to others (such as arts or mathematics). While this is an important step towards local decision-making and thus greater democracy in the education system, it also calls for more precise quality control mechanisms, and for guidance to schools to prevent disparities in educational choice. Finally, schools have some local flexibility in allocating teaching time, which creates more opportunities for offering cross-curricular work and integrated themes as projects for students.

Standards and student achievement

The greatest practical value of the "Yellow Book" lies in its clear formulation of expected learning outcomes. In other countries, "standards" are often no more than a set of requirements for basic curriculum content, a list of what should be covered by subject and by grade level. In Latvia, the "Yellow Book" standards include explicit learning outcomes for students completing Grades 3, 6 and 9. They are formulated for each of the four educational "spheres" (Language, Self & Society, the Arts, and Natural Sciences), in terms of what each student is able to do rather than what he or she "knows" or remembers. In the sphere of Language, for example, 6th-Graders are expected to demonstrate the following communication skills.

The student is able to:

- Speak clearly and express in writing his/her thoughts, feelings, needs and those of others, and understands what others have said and written. .

- Write different texts, taking into consideration the audience.

- Explain, reason about, and defend his/her own thoughts, views, experiences both orally and in writing.

- Verify the credibility of obtained information (*e.g.*, the credibility of a literary plot, media information, or the story of a friend).

In Natural Sciences, 6th Graders are expected to:

- Perform simple observations and practical research, describe the flora and fauna of his/her environment, and recognise general groups of plants and animals.

77

- Understand the main natural processes of living things, and acknowledge the value of life.

- Describe the simplest characteristics of substances and materials used every day, and understand how these characteristics make them useful in everyday life (*e.g.*, food, clothing, school supplies, etc.).

- Understand and explain the change of day and night, length of day, night and year and their relation to the movement of the Earth around the Sun, and have an elementary notion of the solar system.

Such straightforward expectations are valuable to teachers in setting their own teaching objectives, and in motivating their students to achieve the compulsory National Standards. For example, if a student is expected to be able to formulate and defend ideas before a group of classmates, then there should be opportunities for discussion and debate. If a student is expected to be able to do practical research into the flora and fauna around his/her home or school, then there must be time on the timetable for such work, and classroom assessments should take field-work into account as well as classroom performance.

The team endorses the simplicity and spirit of these expectations; if taken seriously, they will have a profound impact on the management of teaching and learning in Latvia's schools.

Assessment and examinations

Status

Continuous assessment of student progress is carried out by teachers in classrooms, using a grading scale of 1-10 (10 = highest). Teachers are guided by national education standards for all subjects, introduced in 1992 but now to be replaced, at least for the nine years of basic (*pamat*) schooling, by the new Standards contained in the "Yellow Book" (MoES, 1998), which set out learning outcomes for students completing Grades 3, 6 and 9.

Under the new system, students in Grades 1-3 do not receive formal marks or grades; their teachers provide oral and written reports describing each child's progress in knowledge, skills, attitudes, development, and class participation. At the end of Grade 3, there is a state test of general learning, first language, and Latvian for children in minority schools. There will soon be new-style tests linked to expected learning outcomes specified in the "Yellow Book", covering creativity, analytical and critical thinking, moral and aesthetic skills, social skills like co-operation, language and mathematical skills, and practical application of learning. For Grade 4, the 10-point scoring system is used for mathematics and language, along with non-graded reports for all other subject areas. Grades 5-9 use the 10-point scoring system for all subjects except social studies, where a "complete/incomplete" designation is used. State tests are again set at the end of Grade 6 (in first language, mathematics, and Latvian for children in minority schools).

At the end of Grade 9, there are both formal state examinations – in mathematics, first language and Latvian for students in minority schools – and compulsory tests in four subjects, two of which are reported to the schools at the start of the academic year and the other two no later than April of that academic year. The size of the cohort at this point is about 33 000 (1998).

Grade 9 graduates receive atestats par *pamatizglitibu* (basic education certificates). General secondary schools are normally required to admit any holder of the nine-year certificate who lives in the school's catchment area, although a gymnasium or other prestigious or specialised school (such as an Art school) may have additional entrance requirements.

Examinations at the end of Grade 12 are set at two levels, basic (*pamatkurss*) or "profile" (*profilkurss* or advanced). Students must take exams in at least five (compulsory core + optional) subjects plus any specialised ones related to the type of school or the student's intended course of further study. The size of the cohort at this point is about 18 500 (1999).

All state exams are set by the MoES's Curriculum Development and Examinations Centre (*Izglitibas Satura un Eksaminacijas Centrs* (ISEC) but are, with some exceptions (see below), marked by teachers in schools. In addition, state examinations used for diagnostic purposes (sometimes called "state control papers") may be given in any subject for any grade level, to give the MoES an overview of student achievement; these are not "exams" which students can pass or fail, but diagnostic tools to assess problems or achievements in a given subject.

New developments

A national, centrally-marked testing system is under construction, focussed in the first place on Grade 12 examinations but with the intention, possibly financed by the World Bank Project, to expand to Grade 9 exams and in the longer term to national tests at Grades 4 and 6.

At the time of the team's visit, centrally-marked Grade 12 tests already existed in English, mathematics, German, French and Russian. Central setting and marking is to be gradually introduced over the next six years, until by the year 2005 about 23 subjects – including core, optional and free-choice – will be centrally set and marked.

One stimulus for a more rigorous and objective approach to measuring student achievement was Latvian students' relatively poor performance on the Third International Mathematics and Science Study (TIMSS) in the mid-1990s. Out of the 41 countries participating around the world, Latvian 13-14 year olds ranked 30th in mathematics and 32nd in science. To confine comparisons to the nine participating Central and Eastern European countries, Latvia came 7th out of 9 in mathematics and 8th out of 9 in science.[12] This disappointing showing indicates that Latvian youngsters, contrary to popular belief, are not achieving as well as their contemporaries in other countries, including those with a recent history similar to that of Latvia. By 1996, the Ministry accepted that the curriculum and assessment methods needed more than piece-meal change – they needed fundamental reform.

Two main reasons can be suggested for this delay. First, there was a lack of experience in the field. Latvia still has no institution for educational research, and universities for many years had paid almost no attention to educational measurement. Initial post-1991 reform efforts, such as they were, relied heavily on borrowings from the West but were not rooted in Latvia's own traditions and values. Second, there was (and is) a widespread belief that education under communism, especially in maths and science, was essentially of world-class quality. Conflict was thus inevitable between the recognition that curricula were heavily content-based and inappropriate to modern life, and a reluctance to remove large areas of syllabus content that had long been associated with high standards. The initial enthusiasm for everything new from other countries gave way to a defensiveness about the existing system, querying whether there was any need for significant change after all. Evidence for the quality of education is often given in the form of maths Olympiad performances, or the exceptionally high performance by students from prestigious specialised gymnasia; but, as TIMSS results show, average Grade 8 students in average Latvian schools lag behind their counterparts elsewhere.

The Olympiad mythology has now made way for a more realistic view of educational quality. In terms of student assessment, the main catalyst was a 1994 initiative by the British Council-Baltics to reform the English language examination at the end of Grade 12. This "Year-12 English" project, covering all three Baltic States, served as the model for similar reforms in other subjects.

Prototypes of new-style tests, and training for assessment specialists and question setters, are still supported by the British Council and the Scottish Qualifications Authority (SQA) in a follow-up project called "Testing Across the Curriculum" which covers Estonia as well as Latvia. In 1998, new-style, centrally-marked examinations were held in English, German, and French; Russian was piloted in 1998, and were intended to go "live" in 1999. Four more pilots (Latvian as a second language, mathematics, algebra and geometry) may be launched in 1999 and conducted "live" in 2000. A phased plan has been drawn up, aiming at having all 23 subjects centrally-set and marked by 2005. However, finances are tight and it may be difficult for ISEC to stay on schedule.

The new examinations emphasise proficiency (mastery) rather than achievement. The distinction here is important in that proficiency tests assume that for a candidate to show "proficiency", he or she must score at least a pre-set percentage of the marks available. In other words, a proficiency test is based on a set of expectations, similar to those set out (for compulsory Grades) in the "Yellow Book". The shift from achievement to proficiency tests has been well received by students and generally also by teachers, although the team heard that some teachers find the tests "difficult" and have problems adjusting their teaching styles. Textbooks, too, were said to be a barrier to change, in that most are still content-heavy and memory-based.

Acceptance by universities is another potential barrier. Some universities are supportive of the new, centrally marked exams and would in principle be willing to accept their results in place of university entrance exams; but some faculties – especially the popular ones where applicants exceed places – insist on setting their own selective entrance tests. If these tests remain heavily knowledge- and content-based, there is a risk that teachers will prepare students for the old-style (high-stakes) university exams rather than for the new-style (lower-stakes) Grade 12 leaving exams. Such powerful but negative "backwash" into teaching and learning in Grades 10-12 could be a serious obstacle to change. It is therefore essential to involve university faculties in the design of ISEC's centrally-marked school-leaving tests, to engage their support and understanding. At the same time, Grade 12 exams are for all school-leavers – approximately 17 000 in 1998 – across the ability range, not only for the smaller group (approximately 65% of graduates of general secondary schools) intending to enter higher education. Young people entering vocational programmes or the job market are also entitled to reliable and valid qualifications, reflecting skills useful to employers or non-university training. Indeed a recent declaration by the Cabinet of Ministers states that, "Every young person shall have a basic education as well as receive the basic professional qualification to be able to stand competition in the changing labour market, including the European Union labour market." [13]

The Curriculum Development and Examinations Centre (Izglitibas Satura un Eksaminacijas Centrs, ISEC)

Curriculum reviews were undertaken very early after Latvia's independence, and a system of national standards was introduced in 1992. These first documents, however, were essentially "content and time-table standards" for each subject, aimed at de-politicising and modernising the curriculum but without a strong conceptual framework. A 1995 revised version began to set out curriculum objectives and expected student outcomes, but radical re-structuring did not start until 1996, culminating in ISEC's 1998 National Standards of Compulsory Education Grades 1-9 (the "Yellow Book").

In the interim, ISEC itself had grown into a strong professional centre directly responsible to the Minister, becoming in effect the "engine room" of educational reform. On the assessment side, it had become clear that Latvia's existing school-based system needed to be replaced by more professional, comparable and independent assessment of student learning, linked not only to the new national standards but also to international ideas about educational quality.

Under the previous system, schools conducted two kinds of formal examinations – oral and written. Questions for the written exams were set in the Ministry and announced on television on the day of the examination, but students' answers were marked by their own teachers. The Ministry also set topics for the oral examinations, but orals were conducted by teachers in their own schools under the supervision of a school-based examination committee. Because no marking schemes were provided and no attempt was made to co-ordinate marking among teachers or across schools, examination results were unreliable and the Ministry could not get an accurate national picture of how well students were doing.

The successful British Council-Baltic States "Year-12 English" initiative (see above) led to plans to extend this model across the curriculum, phasing in centrally-marked Grade 12 examinations year by year until 23 subjects are covered by 2005. However, funding to sustain the gradual expansion of these new exams over the next few years is not assured, especially since ISEC is not only responsible for the nearly 18 000 candidates at Grade 12 but also for the approximately 33 000 students sitting their compulsory Grade 9 examinations. There are also plans to introduce centrally-marked testing at Grades 4 and 6 in relation to the new national standards.

While the team was impressed with the professionalism and efficiency of ISEC's assessment work, there is concern about its heavy workload in relation to its limited size and experience. A number of professional, technical and financial issues also arise.

For example, there is the issue of students' "opportunity to learn". Even a technically perfect, "modern" question paper can be unfair if students have not had an opportunity to learn the skills it asks for. For example, if high marks are given for critical thinking, analytical skills, or communicative skills, students must have had a chance to acquire and practice those skills in the classroom or the results cannot be valid. Careful pre-testing on a representative sample of students will highlight discrepancies in expectations and classroom practice, but more must be done to bring the two in line.

Second, the team is concerned that no "peaceful co-existence" may be possible between the new-style, centrally marked exams and the old-style ones that will need to continue until 2005. It is not simply a matter of central marking versus school-based marking; there are fundamental differences in the types of skills expected of students and therefore in the teaching/learning styles required. While there are good (resource) reasons for the slow pace of change, it could be argued that speedier introduction would minimise confusion and bring benefits more quickly to students already in school now.

Another technical issue pertains to the quality of the test instruments. The subject specialists recruited by ISEC to serve as test-setters were selected, to a large extent, because they were good teachers and were now expected to do at national level what they had done well at school level: interpret the subject curriculum in terms of what students should be able to do and prepare questions to test these things. A subject group supports each ISEC subject specialist. These groups typically consist of five subject teachers from city schools, five from rural schools, and five from higher education. However, no systematic training has been given to these groups, and they have had very limited exposure to testing practices in other countries. The exception is English at "Year-12" and some short workshops conducted by foreign consultants under British Council auspices.

Consequently, ISEC's question papers vary in technical quality, and in some cases, their level of difficulty may be set too high. For example, the 1998 Grade-12 *profilkurss* exam in Algebra asks for a number of extremely unusual algebraic manipulations. Logarithms to bases other than e or 10 are very rare in practice (except base 2 for computing). The questions, as posed, seem to be one-step, without development from one step to another; the question style is totally different from that used in international examinations. (On the other hand, if most Latvian 18-year-olds are expected to manage these questions, their preparation is certainly more thorough than what is required in, say, the UK!). Training and exposure to international practice would help overcome these problems.

Financial issues pertain mostly to the funding and staffing of ISEC itself, but also to the question of cost recovery through the charging of examination fees. The cost to the candidate of a centrally marked ISEC paper is 2.7 lats (approximately US$ 4.50) per subject. This covers question setting, in-house printing at ISEC, distribution, exam supervision, marking, analysis, and reporting of results. The running costs of ISEC are estimated at about 128 000 lats (approx. $576 000) per year. Considering the small number of candidates thus far sitting the new exams (13 000 in 1998), the examination function in the Ministry is relatively expensive, and the costs are not now covered by candidate fees. Although economies of scale will be achieved as numbers rise, the Ministry may need to consider alternative ways to recover costs (for example, from municipalities) without raising the cost to candidates.

However, the cost of reliable and valid measurement of student outcomes after nine or 12 years of schooling is still only slightly more than the cost of a single textbook. The team considers this excellent value for money, well worth the resources devoted to ISEC's development.

Teachers

Since this is a review of education policy, its main focus is on "macro" issues rather than on the conditions in this or that specific school or institution. However, we know that for reform to be successful, it must start with the conditions of people: what are the realities for families and teachers, and for children and young people? How can these conditions be understood and improved? "Reform", in other words, must be rooted in the realities of life in Latvia now.

These realities are real enough, and are well understood especially by people working at the "chalk face" of educational delivery – the teachers. The crucial role of teachers in Latvia's transformation may be obvious; but the burdens placed on them are not always appreciated by reformers. Teachers are expected to adjust not only to new issues but also to new teaching methods. They are expected to become accountable for the quality of schooling, participate in whole-school planning, and be able to implement new technologies in their teaching. They are told they should think differently about learning, knowledge, intelligence and the concept of "school" than they did before. All these issues and many more are facing Latvian teachers, in addition to their difficult material circumstances. The team acknowledges this, and affirms that the stresses placed on teachers by continuous change must be taken into account when education policies are reviewed.

Salary issue

The basic funding formula for teacher salaries is set out earlier in this chapter, along with the observation that financing is insufficient and that there are growing disparities between municipalities that are able to supplement teachers' salaries and those that are not. Here, we are concerned with the impact of low salaries on the quality of the school system.

It would be too simple to argue that money alone is the solution to the problems of schools in any education system. However, in Latvia the low level of financial compensation of teachers' work strongly affects the system, and is particularly acute in the context of fundamental education reform. It is easy to understand that teachers do not greet new demands and requirements with joy when their own living conditions are at stake. While it may be possible to maintain existing structures and practices, it is unrealistic to expect that teachers can summon up the enthusiasm needed to renew their teaching and their schools if their salary level remains well below what the very basic routine workers receive.

Therefore, the level of teachers' pay is a key issue in education policy for Latvia. Teachers in primary and upper secondary schools are currently paid at approximately 75% of the average monthly wage. Teachers in higher education institutions receive salaries that are only slightly better. Given the level of living expenses, especially in the urban centres, teachers have to seek a secondary income after school, or take heavier teaching loads in their own schools. This, in turn, will jeopardise teachers' ability to take part in school-based development work.

How much a teacher is actually paid is determined by a formula that sets the basic salary on a workload of 21 weekly teaching periods. Depending on professional qualification and working experience, the monthly salary varies from 46 to 77 lats. When the teaching load exceeds 21 hours, the salary is proportionately increased. The average workload of Latvian teachers is circa 1.3 times the basic level. This means that, mathematically, there are about 41 000 teachers but in reality they are only about 37 000. Consequently, teachers' salaries are raised artificially by increasing the teaching load from 21 to 27 teaching periods.

It is evident that the low salary level of the Latvian teachers remains a major obstacle to national education reform, despite frequent promises of salary improvements during each state budget negotiation. At the time of writing, there is support in the MoES for doubling the salaries of teachers in higher education, and giving an approximate increase of 50% to basic and secondary school teachers. Meanwhile, some urban municipalities have introduced their own additional salary packages, without waiting for the government to increase the salary budget. For example, in Riga the school board approved a 25% increase in 1998, and another 30% in 1999. This is intended to act as an incentive for school principals to attract and retain good staff, but it also highlights the growing gap between richer and poorer communities.

For Latvia as a whole, low salary levels have serious consequences for educational quality. For example, they discourage young people from entering the teaching profession; they deflect newly trained teachers from entering schools, especially those trained in foreign languages or technology; and they decrease professional status and morale. Young teachers are likely to look for other jobs with better compensation; those who stay often need to carry a second job, and are unavailable for – or unwilling to attend – much-needed in-service training or after-school activities.

Professional competence issues

About one-third of the teachers in primary and general secondary schools lack formal professional qualifications or teach subjects in which they have not been formally trained. Low salaries, low status and a reluctance of well-trained graduates to enter the teaching profession have led to a shortage of qualified teachers, especially in some subjects and geographical areas. The team was told that only about half of all graduates of teacher education institutions take teaching jobs in schools. The teaching cadre is ageing; many serving teachers are near retirement, while there are not enough young teachers – with recent training in modern methods – to take their place.

There is substantial variation in the provision of qualified teachers from one *rajon* and *pagast* to another, and from one subject to another. Urban centres often have better financial resources, and attract teachers away from poorer areas. Riga, for example, has fewer problems in finding trained teachers than some of the eastern *rajons*. The polarisation of schools into "good" schools and "average" schools is likely to promote this trend. The quality of a school is in many cases judged according to its ability to offer advanced level courses in foreign languages and sciences. Naturally, highly trained teachers are critical to these schools.

Latvia's private sector absorbs approximately half the output of teacher training institutions. In the job market, the professional training teachers receive is well regarded, and the education system often loses those with the best managerial, innovative and creative skills. Retaining good teachers for English, German and computer studies is especially difficult; the business sector can easily offer salaries that are two to four times higher, with better career opportunities and higher status. This situation is of course not unique to Latvia or indeed to transition economies; and in Latvia's case, it may be alleviated by the steep drop in the birth rate combined with the necessity for greater efficiency, which will inevitably reduce the number of teachers required. Nevertheless, true renewal in education will be difficult unless talented and well trained young people are encouraged to enter the teaching profession. Better salaries and career paths would provide such encouragement.

Training of teachers

Pre-service training

Several independent teacher-training institutes in Latvia offer different kinds of pre-service and in-service programmes. For example, at the University of Latvia, two parallel departments – the Faculty of Education and Psychology, and the Institute for Pedagogy and Psychology – provide similar training programmes for teacher candidates. Many teachers seem keen to upgrade their initial degrees to master's degrees. In principle, the new teacher training programmes in Latvia place greater emphasis on the aspects of learning and teaching together with the interplay of educational theories and school practice. Without in-depth analysis of the teacher pre- and in-service programmes available in Latvia, the team had the impression that the thinking reflected in teacher training curricula is still dominated by a psychological view of teaching and learning. Furthermore, the study of curriculum and assessment is almost non-existent. The team fears that the present teacher training programmes do not provide trainees with the skills and attitudes they will need to create learning environments that are in line with the new expectations of the National Standards.

Different institutions emphasise different aspects of the teaching profession. Some concentrate on the scientific nature of teaching, while others focus on practical aspects. Therefore, although teachers' professional degrees may be based on the same numbers of credits, the actual qualitative competence may vary considerably. The team does not wish to speculate on which approach is best for Latvia; however, it is important to create national standards also for teacher training programmes, beyond merely quantitative measures such as credit points and "seat time".

In-service training

Before 1990, all in-service training was provided by a single, central institute under the auspices of the MoES. Teachers were required to attend compulsory, state-funded courses at least once every five years. In 1990, this requirement was abolished, and the funds distributed on the basis of a national competition. A number of organisations began to offer training; some universities and colleges established their own centres, and some school boards, municipalities and individual schools set up their own facilities. Many of the previous institute's functions were taken over by the Institute for Advancement of Education, but after 1994 three separate institutions gradually assumed responsibility for in-service training: (1) the Teacher Training Support Centre (Pedagogu Izglitibas Atbalsta Centrs); (2) the Curriculum Development and Examination Centre (Izglitibas Satura un Eksaminacijas Centrs or ISEC), which deals with training in these areas; and (3) the Centre for Professional and Vocational Education (Profesionalas Izglitibas Centrs), which organises training for teachers in professional and vocational secondary schools Funding for in-service training is limited; in 1996, the state budget allocated 130 000 lats, but in 1997 this was reduced to 102 000 lats despite growing needs. The cost of attendance is now borne primarily by local governments and – if they can afford it – by teachers themselves. Provision is therefore uneven across the country, and many teachers receive no in-service training at all. However, the new Law on Education proposes that each teacher will be entitled to 36 days of paid in-service training every five years; this should improve the situation to some extent. The team would hope that a substantial part of this time would be spent on reform-related training, especially in the principles and techniques of competence-based student assessment.

At the same time, the MoES relies heavily on teacher in-service training as the main route by which it introduces schools and teachers to intended changes in classroom practice. The Teacher Training Support Centre (Pedagogu Izglitibas Atbalsta Centrs, attached to the MoES) is the main institution responding to these needs. But because it is centrally located and has only a small staff, this centre does not have the capacity to deliver all the support services that the system requires. Moreover, the in-service programmes it offers do not focus clearly on the core aspects of modern educational change. The linkage between the centre and supportive research on the effectiveness of training programmes, and a deeper understanding of some underpinning issues, are weak or non-existent. The team recommends that the role of the Teacher Training Support Centre should be strengthened and that its programmes should focus on key elements of modern educational development such as school management and alternative methods of teaching and learning. Other key aspects of education reform, in particular curriculum development and assessment, should be co-ordinated with the work of ISEC to avoid duplication, overload, and "mixed messages" to teachers.

A 1997 needs assessment of teacher in-service education showed that a majority of teachers are eager to receive training, mostly in methodology of their own subjects but almost equally in the evaluation of student learning.[14] The survey also showed that newly qualified teachers need particular help, because their training in universities and pedagogical colleges does not prepare them to manage educational change in their classrooms, and they lack the experience of older teachers. Unfortunately, information about in-service opportunities does not always reach teachers, and when it does, there are practical constraints that prevent them from attending. Seventy-six percent of teachers said they found it difficult to attend courses due to lack of money for transport, meals and materials. Almost all teachers in the survey (98%) said they would welcome school-based training, where possible collaboration with neighbouring schools to keep costs down and improve professional "networking".

Another weak point in the structure of the teacher training system is the lack of scientific research related to effectiveness of training. Most of the teacher pre- and in-training programmes have been designed using external models, or are based simply on what the organisers believe to be "good practice". Experience in many OECD countries shows that teacher in-service can be ineffective and expensive; therefore programmes should be more closely monitored, and the concept of training should be extended beyond the traditional out-of-school seminars and workshops. Good examples of these new models have been created and tested in the Faculty of Science of Education at the University of Latvia. These models also provide interesting cases for scientific investigation by researchers and students.

School principals

School principals are often seen as key players in the overall development of schools. In the best cases, the principal is a powerful educational leader who can make his/her school carry out its development plans; in the worst ones, poor management may lead to resistance to change and isolation of the staff. School principals in Latvia have regional and local councils in which they may meet and exchange views. However, there is no national training system or policy for principals and school administrators. Slovenia is one example of a country that is transforming its education system by establishing, a few years ago, a national "school" where all school heads will be trained during the course of given time period. To ensure that changes intended by the MoES are implemented throughout the system, it is important to create a national strategy and a system for providing principals with continuous management support.

In summary, given the existing teacher training system of Latvia, it will be difficult to provide teachers with the tools they need to respond to Latvia's emerging educational and cultural challenges. Change in teachers' work, particularly in the way the classroom practice is organised, requires more than just additional training. If the MoES wishes to see its goals achieved by 2005, a coherent strategy needs to be developed for supporting teachers and schools. That strategy should combine the efforts of the MoES with the teacher training system of Latvia, and with the innovative development work presently being done in universities and schools.

Gender issues

In OECD countries, on average, schools employ approximately two female teachers to each male teacher. In Latvia the proportion of women in schools is relatively higher – as high as 90% in some *pagasts*. This biased gender ratio tends to affect the salary structure of the teaching profession. Men appear to be more ready to move from poorly paid jobs to other sectors where the compensation is better. It may also be that since teaching is a female-dominated profession at the moment, low salaries seem to be tolerated more than in fields with a more balanced gender distribution. There are consequences for classroom life as well. Some would argue that having more men in school could be helpful socially as well as educationally, for example by providing male role models to young children.

Among principals, however, the gender balance is about even. While this is the case in many countries, it does indicate that career paths still differ for men and women, for a number of well-known reasons – such as traditional attitudes, lack of confidence on the part of women, lower career expectations, and women's domestic responsibilities. Gender issues are not limited to the education sector, and cannot be resolved there; however, the MoES could consider ways to encourage more young men to enter the teaching profession, and more women to take on leadership roles in school management.

Evaluating teacher quality

The team heard that Latvia now has no system for evaluating teaching quality. There are plans to introduce a new teacher evaluation process, more systematic than the informal teacher appraisals now done by school heads and rajon inspectorates. Doubts were expressed, however, about teachers' acceptance of formal appraisal: "Teachers are paid so little and work so hard, they will not take kindly to being evaluated" – especially if teacher appraisals are to be linked with salary or promotion.

There is also some thought of connecting teachers' pay with their students' examination results. Other governments (including the UK) are proposing similar schemes; but because schools differ widely in their resources and their students' backgrounds, the team doubts the fairness and effectiveness of such a link. Strenuous efforts made in the UK over the past few years have failed to find a workable "Value-Added" formula.[15] The intention was to find a statistically valid, operationally simple way of tracking each student's progress relative to predictions based on his/her previous attainment and other performance indicators. While it was possible to construct a "Value-Added" model, its complexity made it unworkable in practice. More important, for our purposes, is the confusion of correlation with causation. Strong associations (for example, between good teaching and high examination marks) do not, in themselves, prove that one element causes the other. UK researchers found that large classes often produced better "value-added" results than small classes. Can we then conclude that large classes cause high achievement, or is it that less able students tend to be taught in smaller groups while the high achievers are in larger ones? Introducing results-related pay for teachers, even on a voluntary basis as is now being proposed in the UK, is likely to be highly contentious, and the team would not advise such a policy for Latvia.

Assessment training for teachers

Traditionally, Latvian teachers evaluate their own students through classroom questioning, short tests, and regular end-of-term and end-of-year tests. For the most part, these evaluations are based on the lessons given and the chapter(s) studied in the textbook. However, the team found that pre-service teacher training programmes in Latvia give very little attention to reliable and valid student assessment, although there are now plans to revise teacher training study plans and pay more attention to assessment. Because teacher training programmes are standardised across Latvia, it would be helpful if the study of student assessment could be included in the compulsory (standard) part of the teacher training curriculum, so that all new teachers have up-to-date understanding of modern types of educational measurement.

For serving teachers, almost no in-service assessment training has thus far been available. The introduction of new, performance-orientated curricula and competence-based external examinations has made teachers uncertain about how to assess their students' progress against these new expectations. Until now, classroom questioning, tests and exams were fact-based and norm-referenced, resulting in marks on a 10-point scale (10 = highest), awarded mostly for "reproductive" achievement rather than competence. Teachers are used to this system and find it difficult to think about assessment in a different way. There is an urgent need here for teacher in-service training and also for increased attention to assessment in pre-service teacher training institutions.

Recommendations

1. Translate the new National Standards into the language of practice. Build a supporting structure underneath the new National Standards, including standards for every subject and Grade.

2. Develop Standards for post-compulsory (Grades 10-12) education, and involve representatives from higher education and from the world of work. This would ensure a better "fit" with their requirements, and improve acceptance of new-style qualifications.

3. Ensure that Standards for schools under the jurisdiction of other Ministries – for example, the Ministry of Culture or the Ministry of Agriculture – do not differ substantially from those set by the MoES. For this, it is useful to have MoES representation on Standards working groups in other sectors.

4. Devise a comprehensive system for the regular evaluation and improvement of school quality. The proposed self-assessment and accreditation process will help, but school improvement requires expert support from, for example, a revitalised, professional inspectorate at rajon level. However, the team would caution strongly against any direct link between students' exam results and teachers' performance evaluation or pay.

5. Make the study of curriculum development and student assessment a compulsory part of pre-service teacher training, so that all new teachers have up-to-date understanding of "curriculum" and "educational measurement" in contemporary schooling.

6. Align textbooks with the expectations of the new standards. Textbooks based on the old standards are a barrier to classroom change. An entire new generation of textbooks may be needed. The team accepts the MoES's resource limitations, but unless textbooks are revised there is a risk that teaching and learning will remain knowledge-based and subject-bound despite curriculum and exams reform.

7. Ensure that students have fair and sufficient opportunity to learn skills that will be required by the National Standards and by new-style examinations (for example, critical thinking, analytical or communicative skills). Careful pre-testing on representative samples of students will highlight discrepancies between expectations and classroom practice, but more must be done to bring the two in line.

8. Speed up the introduction of centrally marked examinations in all subjects. The team accepts there are good (resource) reasons for the slow pace of change, faster introduction would minimise confusion and bring benefits more quickly to students already in school now. Increase financial and human resources to support ISEC. The MoES may need to consider alternative ways to recover costs (for example, from municipalities) without raising the cost to candidates.

9. Create a strategy for utilising research in developing education in Latvia, and encourage better communication between administrators, researchers, innovators, and teachers, especially by upgrading the research and education reform capabilities in the MoES and local education administration.

10. Formulate a more comprehensive policy response to the issues of declining birth rates and longer-term efficiency of schools, especially in rural areas. For example, an alternative would be to a transfer from a system of 4 + 5 in basic education to 6 + 3 in order to make it easier to retain small rural schools.

11. Re-establish the extension of compulsory schooling to the pre-school level for all 6 year olds, provided that poorer municipalities receive some extra support to assume this responsibility.

12. Devise a national strategy and training system for principals and school administrators, to provide them with continuous management support and to ensure that changes intended by the MoES are implemented throughout the system.

13. Make every effort to raise the level of teachers' pay. Low salaries and poor career prospects have serious consequences for educational quality.

14. Improve and rationalise the pre- and in-service system. If the MoES wishes to see its goals achieved by 2005, a coherent strategy is needed to support teachers and schools. The present system is unlikely to provide Latvia's new and serving teachers with the tools they need.

15. Intensify in-service training work, improve its funding and co-ordination, and deliver seminars as close to school-level as is practical. Focus on whole-school, locally-targeted work, instead of external seminars that have less impact on school change, require teachers to travel, and take them out of their classrooms more than necessary. Provide printed teacher support materials (handbooks, guides, sample tests etc.) to back up training.

Notes

1. Law on Education, Article 4.

2. MoES, Education in Latvia, 1995/96 to 1998/99, p. 8. Riga: 1999.

3. The World Bank, Republic of Latvia' "Education Sector Strategy Paper" Washington: August 1998, p.7.

4. There is no officially approved definition of "comprehensive" in this context. The common understanding, however, is that "comprehensive schools" are those that go all the way from Grade 1 to Grade 12, but not vocational, professional or special schools. An approximate translation for "comprehensive schools" is visparizglitojosas skolas.

5. MoES, Education in Latvia, 1995/96 to 1998/99, pp. 8 et seq. Riga: 1999.

6. MoES, Education in Latvia, 1995/96 to 1998/99, p. 12. Riga: 1999.

7. Republic of Latvia, Central Statistical Bureau, Education Institutions in Latvia at the Beginning of School Year 1998/99, pp. 40-43. Riga: 1998.

8. Ibid. p. 16. Riga: 1999.

9. The World Bank, ECSHD. "Project Appraisal Document (and Annexes) on a Proposed Loan to the Republic of Latvia for an Education Improvement Project". Washington: January 19, 1999.

10. Centre for Curriculum Development and Examinations (ISEC), National Standards of Compulsory Education Riga: 1998. MoES, pp. 4 et seq.

11. ibid. p. 12.15.

12. Péter Vári, ed. Are We Similar in Math and Science? A Study of Grade 8 in Nine Central and Eastern European Countries. Budapest: IEA/TIMSS, 1997, pp. 106-107. CEE countries participating included Bulgaria, Czech Republic, Hungary, Latvia, Lithuania, Romania, Russian Federation, the Slovak Republic, and Slovenia.

13. Cabinet of Ministers, "Declaration of the Proposed Activities by the Cabinet of Ministers". Riga: January 1999.

14. Marite Seile, "The Situation in Latvian Teacher In-Service Education: Needs Assessment", p. 21. Riga: 1997, Soros Foundation Latvia. Mimeo.

15. School Curriculum and Assessment Authority and the University of Durham. The Value-Added National Project: Final Report. Feasibility Studies for a National System of Value-Added Indicators. London: 1997.

Chapter 4

Vocational Education and Training

Policy structure and governance

The Law on Vocational Education and Training was enacted in June 1999. The purpose of this Law is to ensure the implementation of national policy of vocational education and the functioning, management and development of the vocational education system. The aims defined in the law are to:

- Ensure opportunities to acquire general knowledge and skills, as well as professional qualifications.

- Determine the stages and levels of vocational education and the education required before obtaining the respective professional qualifications.

- Determine responsibility of the persons involved in vocational education and their authority to award professional qualifications.

- Ensure the compatibility of vocational education and professional qualifications received in the Republic of Latvia with the corresponding vocational education and professional qualifications acquired abroad, enabling students to continue their education abroad and to be competitive on the international labour market.

The Law on Vocational Education and Training regulates basic vocational education, secondary vocational education and the first level of higher professional education, and the awarding of the relevant professional qualifications. The Law on Higher Education Establishments and other laws and regulations regulate the second level of higher professional education and the awarding of the relevant professional qualifications.

The Law on Vocational Education and Training provides that the Cabinet of Ministers sets the policy and adopts a strategy of vocational education, sets occupational standards and approves regulations of colleges. The Cabinet of Ministers also establishes the procedure for organizing field practice, specifies the officially recognized forms of professional qualifications documents, and sets the criteria and procedure of issuing such documents.

The MoES authority related to vocational education and training is to:

- Develop model regulations for vocational education institutions.

- Create and update the register of occupational standards.

- Work out proposals and request the assigning of state budget resources in the prescribed procedure and finance the vocational education establishments under its supervision and vocational education support organisations from the funds allocated for these purposes.

- Draft regulations for organizing field practice and draft other legislation in the sphere of vocational education.

Table 7. **Vocational Education Budget By Supervising Ministries, 1998**

| Ministry | Total budget | Out of which | | | | |
| | | Subsidies from the general income (the State budget) | | Own income | | |
	mil. Ls	mil. Ls	%	mil. Ls	%
Ministry of Education and Science	12.87	11.09	86.17	1.78	13.83
Ministry of Agriculture	11.64	8.95	76.89	2.69	23.11
Ministry of Welfare	1.65	1.58	95.76	0.07	4.24
Ministry of Culture	2.91	2.77	95.19	0.14	4.81
TOTAL:	29.07	24.39	83.90	4.68	16.10

Source: Academic Information Centre – Latvian National Observatory. From materials of national report on the modernisation of VET System in Latvia to European Training Foundation, 1999, p. 62.

- Organise vocational guidance and research into the development of the labour market and into the demand on the labour market.

Three other ministries – Agriculture, Welfare and Culture – also supervise vocational education institutions. The Law on Vocational Education and Training defines the authority of these ministries to:

- Develop proposals and in accordance with the established procedure request the assigning of state budget resources, finance the vocational schools supervised by them and vocational education support organisations from the funds allocated for these purposes.

- Co-operate with the MoES in developing and updating occupational standards, in assessing the quality of vocational education and in other issues related to vocational education.

- In co-operation with the MoES, other state institutions and local governments organise further education of educators from educational institutions under their supervision.

- Participate in the work of state, municipal, trade union, employers' and other voluntary organisations and in the work of institutions facilitating co-operation.

- Perform all other functions related to vocational education as prescribed by this Law and the Law on Education.

The Law on Education and Training establishes a Vocational Education Co-operation Board that is a public advisory and co-ordination institution consisting of representatives from ministries, municipalities, vocational education institutions, employers' and other voluntary organisations involved in the implementation of vocational education. The objective of the Co-operation Board is to facilitate decision making related to vocational education and to foster co-operation of persons involved in developing and implementing national policy of vocational education.

Financing of vocational education

In 1998, the total budget for vocational education in Latvia was 29.07 million lats. The state budget financed most – 24.39 million lats (83.9%) of this budget. Table 7 shows the vocational education budgets by ministry. Among the other sources of financing are municipalities, revenues generated by the schools

97

in providing services, and, in the case of private schools, student fees. The MoES provides budgetary support for wages and social taxes for vocational schools founded by municipalities, but other costs are borne by the municipalities (*e.g.*, utilities, materials and maintenance).[1]

Changing configuration of vocational education institutions and programmes

Changes since Soviet times

The configuration of vocational education institutions and programmes in Latvia evolved from the highly centralised policies of the Soviet Union. Vocational schools were closely tied to large industrial enterprises and collectivised agriculture. The institutional network was characterised by a high level of specialisation and a large number of small, single profile schools. The collapse of the command economy and other changes since 1990 have had a profound impact on vocational education. The number of professions and specialisations has decreased from over 1 000 in Soviet times to 329 more broadly defined professions. Programmes and enrolments have shifted – and continue to shift – away from those linked to the former economy toward those in demand in the emerging labour market, including business/commerce, services, transport, and communications. Since 1990/91, the number of vocational schools and secondary professional schools has decreased by 14%. These changes have resulted from the 1993 reorganisation of specialised secondary teacher-training schools as higher education institutions, the merger of small, single profile schools and the emergence of private schools.

New definitions and classifications

As enacted in 1999, the Law on Vocational Education and Training sets forth important definitions for different dimensions of the vocational education system in Latvia. These include the stages of professional education, levels of professional qualification, names of different institutions, and the types of vocational education programmes.

Stages of professional education

The Law defines three stages of professional education: vocational basic education, vocational secondary education, and higher professional education. Higher professional education is further divided between the first higher level of professional education and the second level of higher professional education. As indicated above, the second level of higher professional education is regulated by the Law on Higher Education Establishments.

Levels of professional qualification

The Law further defines five levels of professional qualification:

- Level I – theoretical and practical training enabling a person to perform simple work in a specific sphere of practical activities.

- Level II – theoretical and practical training enabling a person to perform qualified work independently.

- Level III – advanced theoretical training and professional craftsmanship enabling a person to fulfil specific executive tasks including planning and organisation of the work to be performed.

- Level IV – theoretical and practical training enabling a person to perform complicated executive work, as well as to plan and organise the work of other professional.

- Level V – the highest qualifications of a professional in a specific branch enabling him/her also to plan and to carry out scientific research in the respective field.

Names of institutions and types of vocational education programmes

Vocational education institutions governed by the provisions of the Law on Vocational Education and Training are to be named schools, secondary schools, or colleges in accordance with the level of education provided. The types of programmes are classified into programmes of basic vocational education, vocational training, vocational secondary education, the first level of higher professional education, and programmes of further vocational education.

In 1998/99, there were a total of 120 vocational education institutions, including 74 vocational schools (*arodskola*) and 46 secondary professional education institutions (*videja speciala izglitiba*) (Figure 10). Schools also exist for persons with special needs These include a State Rehabilitation centre for disabled persons with basic and secondary education. The number of vocational schools designed to train disabled or other special needs persons has decreased significantly in recent years. The number of schools in prisons has also decreased and only two such schools currently exist. More than one-third of the vocational education institutions (37%) are located in Riga.

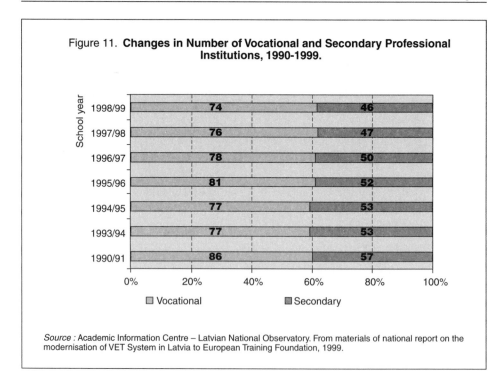

Figure 11. **Changes in Number of Vocational and Secondary Professional Institutions, 1990-1999.**

Source : Academic Information Centre – Latvian National Observatory. From materials of national report on the modernisation of VET System in Latvia to European Training Foundation, 1999.

The MoES has responsibility for the largest number of schools: 53 schools, including 44 vocational schools and 9 secondary professional schools (Table 8). The Ministry of Agriculture has responsibility for 38 schools, including 22 vocational schools and 16 secondary professional schools. The nature of the schools differs among the ministries. Except for four private schools, all the vocational schools (*arodskola*) are under the MoES, the Ministry of Agriculture, or municipalities. In Soviet times, many of these schools not only prepared workers for industrial plants, collective farms, or other state operations but also performed important social functions for youth who did not gain entry into selective general secondary or secondary professional education. In contrast, all the schools that are the responsibility of the Ministries of Culture and Welfare are secondary professional schools – schools that are selective and require a higher level of academic and professional performance.

Not all populations are equally well served. Those at increased risk of educational and social exclusion are women, people below 25 and above 50 years of age, non-Latvian speakers (Russians are the largest ethnic minority in Latvia), and people living in rural areas.

Table 8. **Vocational Schools and Secondary Professional Schools**
Number of schools, teaching staff, and enrolment, 1998/99

Ownership	Number vocational schools (arod-skolas) Enrolment	Enrolment	Teaching Staff	Number secondary professional schools (videjas specialas macibu iestades)	Enrolment	Teaching Staff
MoES	44	18 241	1 598	9	8 411	563
Ministry of Culture				14	1 786	911
Ministry of Agriculture	22	6 621	896	16	6 441	767
Ministry of Welfare				6	1 630	378
Municipalities	4	784	85			
Private	4	595	54	1	163	22
Other					1 565	156
Total	74	26 241	2 633	46	19 996	2 797

Source: Republic of Latvia, MoES, Education in Latvia, 1995/96 – 1998/1999. Riga, 1999.

The Rehabilitation Centre in Jurmala is provides vocational education courses for people with disabilities. The centre offers two-week courses on professional guidance and some basic and secondary level vocational programmes for disabled persons. At present, the choice of programmes is limited to business and computer studies.

Students

At the beginning of 1998/99, the total number of students in all types of vocational education and secondary professional institutions was 46 200. Most were studying full time. Between 1996/97 and 1998/99, the number of students increased by 7%. Most of this increase occurred, however, in secondary professional schools.

- In 1998/99, the total number of students in vocational schools (*arodskolas*) was 26 200. Compared to 1996/97, the number of schools decreased by four, including one under the Ministry of Agriculture and three under the MoES. Enrolments decreased slightly.

101

• In secondary professional institutions (*videja speciala izglitiba*), the enrolment in 1998/99 was 20 500. Compared to 1996/97, the number of students increased by 19% and the number of schools decreased by four, including one private school and three schools under the Ministry of Welfare.[2]

Vocational schools enrol primarily youth aged 15 to 19 who attend fulltime. Students attending in the evening or taking correspondence courses constitute less than 8% of the enrolment.

In 1998/99, 18 171 students enrolled for the first time in vocational and secondary professional schools; most (72.7%) enrolled after nine-year basic education. 17.6 % enrolled after general secondary education (*vispareja videja izglitiba*). As one might expect because of their higher level and greater selectivity, secondary professional schools as compared to vocational schools accept a smaller percentage of applicants, and enrol larger numbers of students who have already completed general secondary.[3]

Vocational education enrolments, especially in vocational schools, remain heavily concentrated in engineering programmes. More than half (56.7%) of the vocational school students and 35% of the secondary professional school stu-

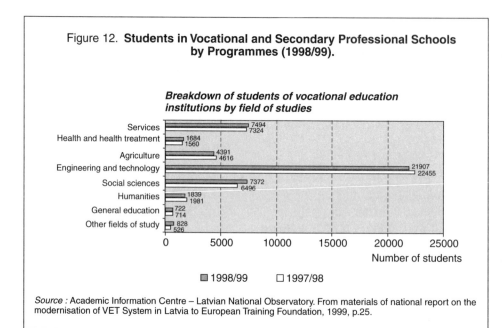

Figure 12. **Students in Vocational and Secondary Professional Schools by Programmes (1998/99).**

Breakdown of students of vocational education institutions by field of studies

Field	1998/99	1997/98
Services	7494	7324
Health and health treatment	1684	1560
Agriculture	4391	4616
Engineering and technology	21907	22455
Social sciences	7372	6496
Humanities	1839	1981
General education	722	714
Other fields of study	828	526

■ 1998/99   □ 1997/98

Source : Academic Information Centre – Latvian National Observatory. From materials of national report on the modernisation of VET System in Latvia to European Training Foundation, 1999, p.25.

dents are in engineering programmes. If the new entrants are an indication of changing demand, slightly fewer vocational school students are entering engineering programmes (55.6%). More vocational school students are enrolling in social science and service professions (30%).

Employment of graduates

Of the 11 4296 unemployed persons registered at the State Employment Service (SES) on 1 October, 1999, 552 (0.5%) were state and municipal vocational school graduates from 1998/99. This number represents less than 0.5% of the graduates. Differences among schools in relation to the total number of graduates suggest significant differences in the ability of recent graduates to enter the labour market. Municipal schools represented only 2% of all vocational school graduates but accounted for the highest percentage (8.7%) of the recent vocational school graduates among the registered unemployed. Graduates of schools under the Ministry of Agriculture represented 5.2% of the registered unemployed, and 24% of the graduates. Graduates of schools under the MoES accounted for 4.9% of the recent graduates who were registered unemployed, but represented 66.5% of the total vocational school graduates.[4]

However, data on unemployed persons registered with the SES may not be accurate indications of the success of recent graduates in the labour market. Since 1995, the number of unemployed vocational school graduates has decreased significantly (as well as the total number of registered unemployed) in part because of changes in the eligibility for registration with the SES. Students who are not eligible for social insurance and do not meet other requirements are not eligible to register.

Language of instruction

Of the 46 237 students enrolled in vocational education at the beginning of the 1998/99 school year, the language of instruction was Latvian for 33 332 (72.1%) and Russian for 12 905 (27.9%) (School year 1995/96 65% Latvian, 35% Russian).

Significant regional differences remain in the extent to which Russian is the language of instruction. The language of instruction is Russian for 6 600 students in Riga, 3 300 students in Daugavpils, and 1 900 students in Liepâja. In Riga, 46% of the students are studying in Russian; in the Latgale region, the number is 40%.

The number of students for whom the language of instruction is Latvian increased from 1995/96 to 1998/99, while the number of students taught in Russian decreases slowly. The most significant increase was in the number of

103

students in secondary professional education whose language of instruction was Latvian.

In schools under the authority of the MoES, 10 167 students (38%) are taught in Russian. In schools under the authority of the Ministry of Agriculture, 1 404 or 11.7% of all students are taught in Russian. Of the students in institutions under the authority of the Ministry of Culture, 49 students (2.7%) have Russian as their language of instruction. Only in professional education institutions under the authority of the Ministry of Welfare is the whole study process carried out in Latvian. Number of students having Russian as a language of instruction in municipal VET schools is 266 (34% out of total number of students in municipal schools) and in private schools- 585 students (77% out of total number of students in private VET schools).[5]

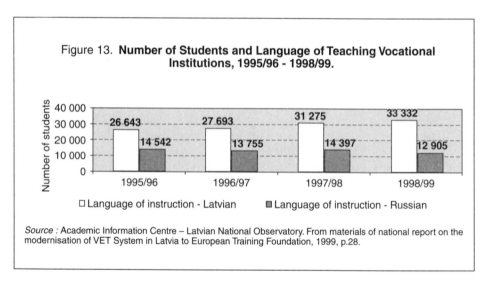

Figure 13. **Number of Students and Language of Teaching Vocational Institutions, 1995/96 - 1998/99.**

Source : Academic Information Centre – Latvian National Observatory. From materials of national report on the modernisation of VET System in Latvia to European Training Foundation, 1999, p.28.

Continuing education and adult training and retraining

Legal and conceptual framework

The 1992 Law on Vocational Training and Requalification regulates retraining for the unemployed. The MoES's concept of adult education stems from the former concept of 'folk [people's] education': the main goal is to provide everyone with the possibility to upgrade knowledge and skills corresponding to individual interests, needs, age, and previous education level. The intent is to compensate for scarcity of education during the transition, and to solve problems of social adaptation and integration. The Ministry of Welfare is currently preparing a new employment policy. This policy will establish new employment structures to better respond to the requirements of EU integration, improve the guidance and counselling system, and provide for financing of active labour market measures. From a lifelong learning perspective, however, there are still major gaps between the concept of adult vocational education and training and the realities of Latvia's institutional and support framework.

Administrative and institutional framework

As with vocational schools and secondary professional education institutions, four Ministries have supervisory or operational responsibilities for continuing training in their sectors. In addition to its operating responsibility, the MoES also has overall co-ordinating responsibility with respect to all continuing training. In practice, the line ministries act independently and with little or no co-ordination. The State Employment Service with the Department of Labour of the Ministry of Welfare is responsible for the training of the unemployed registered with the service.

The Professional Career Guidance Centre under the Ministry of Welfare's Labour Department is the principal organisation responsible for vocational orientation and guidance. The functions of the Centre are to advise students in school and unemployed persons on educational and professional decisions. The Centre also serves as a methodical and co-ordination centre for professional orientation in Latvia. The basic activities of the Centre are student counselling, consultation for the unemployed, co-ordination and teaching work in the field of professional orientation, and scientific and methodological work. The impact of the Centre remains low because of its limited capacity with the result that professional counselling is not accessible to all students. The division of responsibilities for the counselling between the Ministry of Welfare, the MoES, and municipalities is unclear.

The Centre also counsels students of professional and higher education establishments, the employed population, and job seekers. There are six branches – in Daugavpils, Liepâja, Lîvâni, Rezēkne, Gulbene and Valmiera, and there is a mobile consultation unit to help students in rural areas. The Centre plans to open consultative affiliates in all districts of Latvia.

Training for unemployed

The State Employment Service provides training for the registered unemployed. The SES has 67 local/regional offices including in the larger cities and in each rajon. With 547 staff with varying qualifications and a high turnover, the capacity of the SES is limited.

The registered unemployment rate in Latvia has increased from 6.7% (end 1997) to 9.1% (end 1999), with Rezekne district having the highest level (28.2 in the end of 1998%). The impact of the Russian economic crisis following August 17, 1998 contributed to this increase. Only one-third of the unemployed receive benefits, and these benefits are only 50% of the minimum wage. Although 50% of those trained find a job within three months, the SES is able to offer training to only 14.9% of the registered unemployed. The Professional Career Guidance Centre consults unemployed persons, who has a difficulty to choose the training.

The SES selects training providers through an annual tendering process. For 1999, the Service selected 60 such providers out of 90 applicants. Training activities are carried out by many organisations, almost all of which are represented in the Consultative Council of Adult Education. State vocational schools constitute only one-third of the providers and most are private providers. Providers offer training in more than 100 specialities, but the SES does not select training courses based on detailed analyses of potential employment prospects. Instead, the SES matches the requests of the individual unemployed with courses currently on offer. The courses are mainly short-term and do not lead to a qualification that would allow the person to move horizontally or to pursue further education or training. The principal performance criterion for training providers is the employment of trainees. The lack of a common qualification structure for vocational education – and the absence of an accreditation process – are barriers to effective quality assurance.

According to the Language Law, the SES can work only with unemployed persons who know the Latvian language. As mentioned earlier in this report, this restriction limits the number of persons who can officially register with the Employment Service – including graduates of vocational schools who do not know Latvian and who are not eligible for social insurance. Recognising this problem, the SES offers language training programmes. These training programmes enrolled 1 000 participants in 1995.[6]

Financing

Funding in 1997 for continuing education and adult training and retraining included:

- State expenditure (43.2%)

- Tuition fees paid by the learners (17.5%)

- Funding from firms and organisations (35.2%)

- Municipal budget (1.9%)

- Other sources (2.2%)

- Funding provided for labour market training is approximately 4.3 million lats. Investment of employers into staff training has than tripled in comparison with the periods 1995 and 1998.

Status of reform and policy issues

Vocational education reform process

In the first phase of the vocational education reforms (1995-98), the emphasis was more on developing the legal frameworks than on policy design and implementation This phase culminated in the Law on Vocational Education and Training enacted in June 1999.

The present Government has identified education as one of its priorities, and the MoES is committed to the reform of the vocational education system. However, the policy tools and resources remain limited for effective implementation.

The second reform phase, which began in 1999, is driven by the requirements of EU accession. It should bring together all vocational education initiatives under a common framework. The development of strategies is proceeding in this direction. A major need is for a transparent national qualification structure responding to labour market demands. Other issues are: lack of a vocational teachers' and trainers' training programme; development of continuing training; and strengthening of a vocational education research capacity. The ETF-sponsored Latvian National Observatory could assist the ministries in narrowing the gap between the employment system and education; the Observatory has developed useful quantitative and qualitative labour market monitoring techniques, and are involved in an Employment Background Review.

Role of external assistance

External assistance has played a dominant role in the reform of the Latvian vocational education system. In the country's severe economic conditions, 97% of the state budget for vocational education has been committed to teachers' salary costs and school maintenance, with only 3% devoted to innovation. The government initially welcomed all assistance from the European Union as well as foreign bilateral initiatives without much attention to the possible overlap of outcomes and different approaches of donor counties and organisations.

Almost the entire vocational education and training reform has been financed by EC-Phare VET Reform Programmes (altogether 7.0 million euro), European Union (EU) and European Training Foundation (ETF) funded projects, and other donors. Examples of other bilateral and multilateral initiatives are:

- Germany: Support to entrepreneurship in agriculture, development of the MoES Centre of Professional Development, and establishment of commerce training model centres and metal technology centres.

- Denmark and Finland: Creation of a vocational education teacher training system.

- Nordic Council of Ministers: Vocational and technical training in the Baltic countries – information exchange and network building.

Staff training for the Latvian State Employment Service (SES) has been organised mainly with the help of foreign partners from Sweden, the German Federal Ministry of Labour and Social Affairs, the United Kingdom, and the EC-Phare programme.

The EU programmes – Leonardo da Vinci and Socrates – provide opportunities for Latvia to accelerate the building of international partnerships in general secondary education in addition to vocational and higher education. The Leonardo da Vinci programme is project-based at the state level and at the EU for pilot projects for creating teaching materials and methods, student exchange, and research and analysis. For the programme period 1998-2000, the budget for Latvian participation is 2 760 000 euro.

The ETF helps partner countries to enhance the synergy among assistance initiatives to contribute more effectively to the reform of vocational education systems. For example, in Latvia and Lithuania, the ETF is sponsoring a vocational education teacher training project and will act as co-ordinator to draw on the contributions from Denmark, Finland, and Sweden.

Despite the achievements so far under the various pilot projects and ongoing initiatives, the pilot schemes must be anchored to the formal structures responsible for administering the vocational education system. A feeling of shared ownership toward the new procedures is necessary. The different reform initiatives have not been undertaken on the basis of a coherent strategy, as the overall reform policy framework is still being debated.

National and regional policy development and co-ordination

The vocational education system remains centralised, with responsibilities shared between four ministries (Education and Science, Agriculture, Welfare and Culture). At present the roles of different ministries responsible for vocational schools in relationship to the MoES are confused. Actions to strengthen the institutional capacity of the MoES should include regionalisation of vocational education and decentralisation of administrative responsibilities to allow the MoES to focus more on strategy and policy development. Unfortunately, frequent changes in MoES leadership (nine Ministers since 1995) have made consistent pursuit of reforms difficult.

An alternative now under discussion is a plan to strengthen the policy development capacity of the MoES. This would organise administrative tasks outside the ministry, and emphasise regionalisation of education services. Both the separate agency and regionalisation of vocational education schools could lead to better co-ordination of vocational education schools among the four line ministries. Decentralisation of vocational education would also increase the possibility of bringing general and vocational education closer together, and of developing an integrated approach to human resource development at the regional level to respond to regional and local needs.

So far, the vocational education policy development capacity has mainly remained at the Agency for Vocational Education Development Programmes (VEDP – PIAP Agentura), outside the Vocational Education Development Department of the MoES. The EC-Phare VET 2000 programme has a component to strengthen the ministry's vocational education administration and governance, but at present the capacity is still mostly foreign or outside the ministry. The MoES plans to place organisational responsibility for vocational education teacher training, continuing vocational education, and college-level vocational education with the Vocational Education Development Department. This change should facilitate the development of an integrated approach to vocational education.

The future role of the PIAP Agentura will depend on funding. It is important that the Agentura's experience and knowledge of project management and EU programmes not be lost. New activities could be developed – *e.g.*, in management of international human resource development projects or preparation for or actual participation in European Social Fund activities. The Agentura's responsibility for the Leonardo da Vinci programme is in line with this.

There is a plan to turn the Vocational Education Reform Strategy Board attached to the PIAP Agentura into a vocational education council with responsibilities similar to those of the Higher Education Council. At present, the Strategy Board has only an advisory role, but it does include all key vocational education stakeholders (*e.g.*, representatives of social partners and five different ministries).

There is no institutional capacity within the MoES for education and labour market research. The EC-Phare programme and ETF-supported National Observatory have contracted out a series of small vocational education and labour market research projects, but these are insufficient to provide the necessary information for policy development. The SES, in collaboration with the employers' and local governments, carries out its own research on training needs.

Optimising the school network and regional co-ordination

The MoES plans to optimise the school network in order to promote greater efficiency. These changes will inevitably mean closing down some smaller schools and/or establishing regional training centres that are based on the consortium/network approach. The Ministry of Agriculture has already established eight centres specialising in different areas of agriculture and forestry. EC-Phare is piloting two consortium/network-based vocational education and training institutional centres, in the districts of Rezekne and Daugavpils. However, with the existing governance system, there is no flexibility to run such regional centres responding to local labour market needs, because of the large number and small size of the 483 *pagasts* and 26 *rajons*. Significant improvements in regional co-ordination in vocational education will depend on the territorial reform now under consideration.

Differences in governance and financing between general secondary education and vocational education are additional impediments to integration of education and training. Closer co-ordination is also needed among the different local and regional actors in vocational education and training. This is the case for regional training and examination centres, local employment offices, professional career guidance centres, the 26 adult education centres, eight regional agricultural centres, and the other state and private training providers as well as local commerce and industry.

Language issue

The first stages of education reform have attempted to address the legacy of Soviet times of a large proportion of vocational schools where the language of instruction is Russian. By 2004, all teaching at secondary schools at Grade 10 and vocational education secondary teaching will be delivered in the Latvian language. This presents a significant challenge in developing the language skills of existing teachers as well as developing instructional materials in Latvian.

Student demand for vocational education

Since 1991, student demand after basic compulsory education (Grade 9) has been shifting strongly toward general secondary education, and within secondary education toward selective programmes that lead to higher education. Currently 61% of those who complete Grade 9 in 1998 go on to general secondary education, compared to 21% for vocational schools and 12% for secondary professional schools.. Some of this change can be attributed to the lack of relevance of vocational schools and programmes to the changing needs of the labour market. The change also reflects the uncertainty of the labour market in that students and parents perceive a general education to provide more options in a rapidly changing environment. Nevertheless, not all students are successful in gaining entrance to selective programmes leading to higher education. Prior to the enactment of the Law on Vocational Education in 1999, Latvia did not formally recognise "college" level vocational education level. Therefore, students who could have benefited from post-secondary education at a level below university had limited means to obtain a qualification after general secondary education. Consequently, nearly 30% of school leavers enter the labour market without any vocational qualification (6% after 9 year basic education; around 12% leaving secondary general and vocational education without diploma; and 24% as graduates from general secondary education). Those school leavers run the highest risk of becoming unemployed. Hopefully, implementation of the provisions of the Law on Vocational Education will address these issues.

There are no specific measures to address the needs of school leavers after basic education or during secondary education. Dropout rates for 1998 were approximately 13.9% for vocational education schools and 13.8% for secondary vocational education, compared to 3.0% for general education. Specific approaches should be developed to reduce the number of students leaving initial vocational education without qualification. On the other hand, specific training measures are needed for young adults without qualification.

Many vocational school graduates lack practical skills, either because they receive no practical training or because what they do receive is of poor quality, due to their schools' obsolete technical equipment and their teachers' insufficient knowledge of what the labour market requires. The official registration age for unemployment is 15 years. The SES, however, cannot offer training for 15- to

18-year-olds because they can obtain education and training in vocational or other schools. Special programmes have been designed for school leavers up to 25 years of age, but these have not been implemented because of lack of funding.

Adult education, continuing education and lifelong learning

The Cabinet of Minister's Declaration makes no mention of lifelong learning, and an integrated approach to a lifelong learning system has yet to be developed.

At the same time, however, interest in adult education increased by 6.4% in 1997 as compared with 5% in 1995, but adult education in Latvia tends to be disconnected from retraining directly aimed at the labour market. The demand for adult education is greater than the supply; therefore, little competition exists among the limited number of providers.

There is no clear understanding of the potential contribution of continuing education for the development of Latvia, although enterprises and social partners increasingly recognise the importance of human resource development. A national concept for the development of continuing vocational training is still missing, and the MoES does not consider the development of a continuing vocational training as an urgent issue. The study on continuing vocational training in Latvia carried by the National Observatory could be the basis for the development of such a national concept.

Existing vocational schools play a limited role in adult retraining. Students are primarily those who have recently completed basic education at Grade 9 or, to a more limited extent, general secondary education. As indicated earlier, only one-third of the providers of training programmes for the registered unemployed are state vocational schools.

Demographic trends and the projected decline in student numbers completing Grade 9 are likely to force vocational schools to extend their work to continuing training. Such extension would allow the sector to become more knowledgeable about and responsive to changes in the labour market. It would also require retraining of the teachers in adult pedagogy, and providing schools with up-to-date equipment. At present, there are only two institutions in Latvia providing training in adult-pedagogy. In addition, encouraging the schools to become continuing training providers would give teachers more direct contact with enterprises, and vice versa. Schools that offer continuing training could also generate extra-budgetary income, and make better use of their existing resources.

Counselling and guidance

The Professional Career Guidance Centre is a state-owned enterprise under the Ministry of Welfare, serving the unemployed and schools. The Centre collaborates closely with the SES; it has developed an approach that responds well to the needs of different target groups, but the impact remains low because of its limited capacity. The Centre employs only 50 people for the entire country; therefore, professional counselling is not accessible to all students. In 1998, only about 19% of students leaving schools (Grades 9 and 12) consulted the Centre. Special measures are needed for those who do not continue after basic education. The Centre does provide training for teachers in vocational counselling and professional orientation, but obviously this is not sufficient.

Quality and engagement of social partners

Quality in vocational education depends fundamentally on close links with the labour market on the different levels, especially since preparation for the demands of the labour market is a precondition for employability. Because vocational education in Latvia had its origins in a command economy, relevance to the current and developing economy is a major problem. Engaging a new generation of social partners in every dimension of vocational education must be a priority. Social partners can play important roles in identifying developing professions, defining professional qualifications, providing practical (apprenticeship) experiences for students, and providing access to equipment and training materials. The Trade Unions, the Employers' Confederation, and the Chamber of Commerce see vocational education as a priority. These organisations are participating in the new tripartite Co-operation Council on Vocational Education and contributed to the Law on Vocational Education and Training.

Engaging social partners in developing a national qualification system and curriculum development is in an early stage. They have agreed to the establishment of tripartite branch committees to carry out analysis of labour market trends and define occupational standards. These standards, and related curricula development, will form the basis for a transparent national qualification system responding better to labour market challenges. For example, in 1999, the development of occupational standards for the wood products branch will be completed through the EC-Phare Higher Vocational Education Programme. Three more branches will be developed through the EC-Phare VET 2000 programme next year. With the results of these efforts, the MoES can begin to correlate its educational standards more closely with the occupational ones. The government should then be prepared to fund occupational standards development for 12 remaining branches, beginning in 2001. The planned reorganisation of the Centre of Professional Education (CPE) with participation of the social partners will be an important step to ensure a systematic support to this development of a national qualification system.

Social partners can play an important role through placements for students and partnerships with schools. At present these relationships are limited, and incentives are needed to encourage enterprises to establish stronger connections with schools. At the school level, students can participate in practical training through six-month placements in enterprises. Nevertheless, these placements are difficult to realise, particularly away from Riga and in rural areas. The opportunity to use such placements to build partnerships between schools and enterprises is still not developed. Although some schools manage to maintain contacts with local employers who give financial support and provide practical training, only 13% of enterprises have links with schools. Again, incentives should be developed to encourage stronger links.

Quality related to continuing vocational education

No official quality control mechanisms are in place for either training providers or programmes for adults and the unemployed. Existing mechanisms to accredit new vocational education and training programmes are not effective and a new regulatory and institutional framework for accreditation is being established. The Centre of Professional Education (CPE), a subordinated institution to the MoES, approves training programmes for the unemployed, but the institutions that provide the training award diplomas without any external validation. Existing standards/performance criteria are not used. Providers are judged on whether trainees obtain employment, not on the level of skill the trainees have gained. This may lead to short-term employment, but still leave the trainees with few skills to help them compete in the labour market.

Teacher training and retraining

The most urgent objectives are to provide vocational education teachers with pedagogical competencies, and to enlarge their currently narrow technical qualifications. Although the Latvian authorities recognise the importance of pre-service and in-service teacher training for the implementation of reform, the funds allocated in the budget are insufficient to ensure the minimum compulsory in-service training (12 hours per year, 36 hours every three years).

Traditionally, no special training has been available for teachers in vocational education, and at present there is no unified state concept regarding vocational education teacher training. All teachers – whether in vocational education or not – were educated through the same system. The problem for teachers in vocational education is the missing link between the real work environment and schools. Teachers and trainers have practically no opportunities for in-service training at enterprises or possibilities to use new technology. Furthermore, teachers at the vocational schools usually have neither a vocational (higher or secondary vocational) nor a pedagogical (higher) education background.

The new ETF Teacher Training Project for Latvia and Lithuania aims to:

- Support and supplement innovative vocational education and training actions in the field of teacher/training in Latvia and Lithuania;

- Improve the quality of teacher training by changing the identity of schools/vocational institutions and the roles of teachers/teaching personnel;

- Develop innovative teacher training strategies; and

- Establish co-operation in the field of teacher/training among neighbouring countries of Central Europe.

It is difficult to attract good teachers, as salaries are not competitive. A proposed new salary scale should link the level of a teacher's salary to pre- and in-service training and evaluation. This system should provide incentives for a higher level of professional preparation as well as support and incentives for continuing professional development. Since the OECD review, these issues have apparently been addressed in the reform of teachers' salaries.

Regulation of extra-budgetary income

According to the Ministry of Finance, vocational schools can generate income, although there are currently no regulations regarding how these funds are to be used. Schools use any extra income to supplement teachers' salaries, purchase computers, and meet other school needs not adequately funded through the state budget. However, vocational schools argue that any additional school income is deducted from the annual school budget. Regulations are needed to clarify these issues.

Post-secondary vocational education

At the time of the OECD review, the post-secondary vocational education sector appeared highly fragmented with no consistent conceptual and legal framework. Secondary professional education institutions, universities and specialised private institutions were providing various post-secondary courses without a common understanding of the status of the institutions' diplomas, professional qualifications, or standards. The Law on Vocational Education and Training enacted in June 1999 is an important step in clarifying the conceptual and legal framework. For example the Law makes clear the distinction between the first level of higher professional education governed by the Law on Vocational Education and Training, and the second level to be governed by the Law on Higher Education Establishments.

The EC-Phare Business Education Reform Programme (BERiL) in Latvia has developed college level business education programmes and trained teachers and school managers. At the same time, the EC-Phare Higher Vocational Education Reform Programme has developed the framework for a vocational education qualification structure in which the BERiL pilot fits. The MoES approved this qualification structure at the end of 1998, and piloting of college level programmes will continue with the EC-Phare VET 2000 Programme.

Despite the clarification in the Law on Vocational Education and Training, the coherent implementation of higher professional education ("college level") both in universities and vocational education establishments could be a problem because of uncertainties among both employers and students about the precise distinctions between the levels.

A question remains regarding the capacity of the MoES to ensure co-ordination between the two levels of higher professional education. While the MoES has authority to oversee the first level of higher professional education, questions may remain regarding the MoES's authority for second level higher professional education offered by universities that , by law, have substantial autonomy. While technically within the policy oversight of the MoES, universities are autonomous, under the policy co-ordination of the Higher Education Council.

Recommendations

1. Make the reform of vocational education and training a priority for the Republic of Latvia as a critical element of Latvia's overall education reform. In recent years, external foreign initiatives have been the driving force for vocational education reform. Numerous pilot and demonstration projects have prepared the way for change. New concepts, strategies, and laws have been drafted and enacted. What is needed now is a firm commitment by the Government of Latvia to shape the reforms to be consistent with Latvian culture and priorities, and to move from concepts to implementation. The enact-

ment of the Law on Education in June 1999 was a critical step in this process. Now the challenge is to ensure the implementation of that new Law.

2. Strengthen the capacity of the MoES to provide overall policy leadership and co-ordination for vocational education and training in Latvia. Collaboration of the MoES with other ministries that play roles in vocational education and training (*e.g.*, the State Employment Service, and the Ministries of Welfare, Culture, and Agriculture) is important. Nevertheless, the MoES should have the pre-eminent responsibility to lead reform and to ensure overall co-ordination. There is an important distinction between the MoES responsibility for co-ordination and its responsibility to administer schools under its jurisdiction. To play a stronger co-ordinating role, the MoES should:

   • Decentralise administrative responsibilities to the regional and/or school level

   • Reshape and strengthen the competencies of the MoES to emphasise strategy, policy research, quality assurance, and strategic relationships with other Ministries and social partners.

3. Reform the financing of vocational education and training to promote substantially increased efficiency in the use of physical and human resources and to create a more responsible, flexible, and competitive system. Elements of reform should include:

   • Shifting to norm-based per student funding with substantially increased norms for ratios of students to teachers.

   • Increasing the responsibility and flexibility for school managers to make efficient use of resources and to generate extra-budgetary support – within the framework of MoES oversight.

   • Providing financial incentives and technical support for development of regional training centres and networks to ensure access to vocational education and training throughout Latvia – especially in rural areas.

4. Place renewal of the human resources – teachers, school directors, counsellors, and other personnel – at the top of the reform agenda:

   • Restructure and substantially expand Latvia's capacity for preparation of teachers for vocational education and for adult training and retraining.

- Make a commitment to systemic reform of teacher pre-service and in-service education building on the many successful pilot projects under-way in Latvia. Systemic reform should include reform of every dimension of the system: colleges and universities, schools, staff development networks, employers and other social partners, regional training centres, and policies regarding financing and quality assurance.

- Obtain a firm commitment of universities, with the leadership of the rectors and Higher Education Council, to the reform of the university and college roles in preparation and retraining of teachers for vocational and adult education.

- Provide incentives for teachers and schools for professional development, and ensure access to professional development in cities and rural areas outside Riga.

5. Design and implement a new quality assurance system for vocational education and training in Latvia. Latvia has made substantial progress – largely with external financing and technical support – in developing a proposed qualification structure, qualifications assessment schemes, standards, new curricular designs, accreditation standards and process, and many of the other elements of a comprehensive quality assurance system. The process now underway through branch committees and the reorganisation of the Centre of Professional Education are important steps in this process. Significant progress has been made in engaging employers and other social partners in these processes. Again, what is lacking are the governmental commitment and the capacity to move from plans to action.

6. Establish stronger links between general secondary and vocational education. The reorganisation of the MoES in 1999 to place responsibility for both general and vocational education under the same Deputy State Secretary increases the opportunities for this co-ordination. Recommended actions include:

- Reform both vocational education and general secondary education to (1) ensure that all students completing secondary education gain the core knowledge and skills to be competitive the labour market and to (2) counter the serious problem of school leavers (dropouts) with no useable qualifications.

- In developing national standards and curricula for general secondary education, emphasise the core knowledge and skills graduates will need to be successful in the changing labour market.

- Provide students in general secondary education with opportunities for exposure to, if not active participation in, practical work experiences in enterprises – especially enterprises that illustrate developments in the economy (*e.g.*, use of information technology).

- Increase the opportunities for students to move between secondary vocational and professional education and general secondary education.

- Promote regional co-ordination between vocational education and general secondary schools through regional training centres and other means.

- Balance the current trend toward selective general secondary and secondary professional schools and programmes with increased attention to the quality and effectiveness of education for the students who are not served by elite schools.

- Design specific support programmes to serve disadvantaged populations in need of vocational education and training.

- Recognise that long-term strategies to reduce drop outs will require fundamental reform of vocational education to make the programmes and services more relevant to the changing labour market and social conditions.

- Give priority to continuing training for young adults who have left school without vocational qualifications.

- Provide incentives for practical training phases in enterprises should be developed in not only vocational education but also general secondary education. Give incentives to enterprises to engage in partnerships with schools in order to strengthen the preparation of students for the labour market.

- Develop and extend the counselling and guidance system to strengthen professional orientation of both secondary and vocational education. Provide every school leaver with an opportunity to consult the Professional Career Selection Centre.

- Implement the provisions of the Law on Vocational Education and Training related to higher professional education and provide for clear distinctions and effective co-ordination between the first level and second levels for the benefit of students and for clear communications with employers.

- Make lifelong learning a core concept for all education and training in Latvia.

- Develop a national continuing training concept covering all learning that improves the employability of adults who have left the initial education system.

- Ensure access to continuing vocational education, especially for people without qualification.

- Make more systematic use of the existing school infrastructure for continuing vocational training instead of setting up a parallel infrastructure.

- Provide incentives for continuing vocational training in enterprises.

- Extend regional training centres to all regions of Latvia, and make continuing vocational training an integral function of each of these centres.

- Develop opportunities for adults to participate in retraining leading to recognised vocational qualifications.

- Strengthen co-ordination and collaboration between formal and non-formal education providers (for example, youth organisations) in order to promote lifelong learning in practical levels.

Notes

1. European Training Foundation National Observatory. Latvia: National Report on the VET System. Recent Changes, Challenges and Reform Needs. Riga: 1998, ETF-Observatory Unit, p. 53.

2. Republic of Latvia, Ministry of Education and Science, Education in Latvia, 1995/96 – 1998/1999. Riga, 1999.

3. Academic Information Centre – Latvian National Observatory. From materials of national report on the modernisation of VET System in Latvia to European Training Foundation, 1999.

4. Academic Information Centre – Latvian National Observatory. From materials on national report on the modernisation of VET System in Latvia to European Training Foundation, 1999. Republic of Latvia, Ministry of Education and Science, Education in Latvia, 1995/96 – 1998/1999. Riga, 1999, p. 64 and 79.

5. Academic Information Centre – Latvian National Observatory. From materials of national report on the modernisation of VET System in Latvia to European Training Foundation, 1999.

6. Interview with the Director of the State Employment Service and Head of Labour Department, Ministry of Welfare, February 1999.

Chapter 5

Access and Equity
for Latvian Children

Social exclusion issues and education in Latvia

Who is being served?

The question "Who is being served by today's education system in Latvia?" was central to many of the review team's discussions with officials and colleagues at all levels. The focus of the review is on education policy and how it affects the quality of learning. Nevertheless, the realities of life in Latvia today raise wider issues such as the impact of unemployment, poverty, social isolation and marginalisation on access, choice and equity – not only for school-age children, but for out-of-school youngsters, adults and communities in general. If the main purpose of education is to enable each person to live a useful life within a changing society, then a review of education policy must take account of what that society is like, and how social changes affect the content and delivery of educational services. In Latvia, many former linkages between the family, the school, the community and the state have disappeared, and some vulnerable children are falling through the cracks.

Poverty

As Latvia adjusts to her independent status, some of the old social guarantees of Soviet life are replaced by new social risks. Life has become harder, and less secure; families, and children, are under stress. Agriculture and industrial manufacturing sectors are in trouble. The Ministry of Welfare ranks poverty as Latvia's main social problem, resulting in "a rapid polarisation of communities" along economic, social and cultural lines.[1] The effects of poverty on family life, child health and social participation are felt also in the country's schools, in particular in areas hardest hit by economic crisis. Many families live at or below basic subsistence level, barely managing to buy food and pay for utilities such as heat and light, with little left for education, health care, or transport. The team heard that, in some families, a grandparent's small pension might be the only regular cash income: "Suddenly, grandma is the only one who actually has money!"[2]

The main body responsible for social policy in Latvia is the Ministry of Welfare, established in 1991 and merging the previously separate Ministries of Health and of Social Insurance, as well as the Committee of Labour and Social Affairs and the Department of Welfare of the Ministry of Economics. In relative terms, expenditure on social security (including health care) has risen from 12.5% of GDP in 1992 to 18.3% in 1997. However, because of a fall in GDP and to inflation, absolute expenditures have fallen considerably, while the reported number of cases of regular social assistance has risen steeply (from 77 per 10 000 population in 1992 to more than 2 500 in 1995) . Moreover, family assistance is now the responsibility of municipalities, and they are not accountable to the Ministry of Welfare; nor is there any effective collaboration among Ministries to stimulate regional development and ensure equitable levels of provision across Latvia. Although new social protection laws have been enacted and administrative reforms are underway, central Government has neither the means nor the effective power to ensure their implementation. The 1994 Law on Local Governments, combined with the Law on Equalisation of Local Government Finance, channel financial resources for social assistance directly to local governments, effectively leaving the Ministry of Welfare without direct control or oversight over social assistance to families.

As elsewhere in this review, the team urges radical reconsideration of the entire issue of co-ordination, responsibility, and accountability among different levels and branches of government. Funding mechanisms are a mixture of ministerial, regional, semi-independent and local functions, often without adequate public accountability. In practice, the team was told, "decentralisation simply means that more and more people are in charge of less and less money: the consequences of unfunded mandates and non-enforceable laws are borne by those segments of society least able to protect themselves.

Access

In education, a major objective of post-1991 reforms was to improve variety and choice in education. But especially in rural areas, effective choice is severely restricted: "On 40 lats a month income, you don't have any real choice", the team was told. In some rural areas, the secondary agricultural schools – despite questions about their relevance to Latvia's new economic realities – were described to the team as "a light in the darkness", and often the only realistic chance for rural youngsters to receive secondary vocational education. As rural life deteriorates, urban drift brings younger people into towns and cities putting additional pressure on already poor housing stock and social services. In addition, a small but growing number of school-age children are not in school at all, drop out early, or start their schooling late because of family poverty, isolation or a sense of social detachment referred to in many of the team's interviews as "demoralisation".

The team recommends that issues such as the closure of small rural schools or agricultural schools be approached with full attention to the effects of such closures on the social fabric of communities and on the real-life educational prospects of children.

Social exclusion

The issue of social exclusion, however, is not merely a matter of family income or geography. While the Constitution and the laws of Latvia guarantee the basic rights of all permanent residents of Latvia, as well as equal treatment and non-discrimination of all Latvian residents, there are issues of citizenship and language that affect families and children. The language issue is dealt with elsewhere in this report. As for citizenship, this remains a contentious issue especially with regard to part of Latvia's Russian-speaking population. It is encouraging that, following an October 1998 referendum, the Cabinet of Ministers approved changes to the law that will allow the naturalisation of stateless children born in Latvia after independence.

Although the numbers of refugee and stateless children in Latvia are not large, the approval of these changes signals an important change in attitudes and social climate, and a greater awareness of society's obligations towards all children. The United Nations Convention on the Rights of the Child, which came into force in Latvia in 1992, is monitored by a Commission for the Protection of Children's Rights set up jointly by the Ministry of Education and Science (MoES) and the Ministry of Welfare. Children in situations of emergency, or in conflict with the law; disabled children; children living in the streets or otherwise deprived of a family environment; and children belonging to a minority group are – at least de jure – entitled to the Commission's protection. A Children's Rights Protection Centre (1995) under the authority of the MoES independently implements the state functions delegated by law and is responsible for their imple-

125

mentation. However, the team believes that thus far its work has been limited to providing information and advice about legal instruments rather than active advocacy of children's educational rights.

One major problem is the lack of a reliable, co-ordinated register of all children of school age in Latvia: in fact there are now three separate registers each showing different numbers of children. The problem apparently lies in an out-dated system of registration of residents (registered address of residence) and the co-ordination of activities with the Ministries of Interior and Welfare and municipalities. Decisive steps should be taken to co-ordinate the work of various ministries, departments, and municipalities to create a unified register that provides a firm basis for its key policy and resource decisions. A second problem is a lack of trained and experienced social workers, a profession relatively new to Latvia. There is still little understanding – both at the level of government and among the general public – of the need to support families at risk of breakdown, rather than merely identifying "problem children" and taking them into public care, thereby isolating the child and damaging the family even more. The Ministry of Welfare has put together a "White Paper" outlining social welfare reform and planned legislation, but at the moment there is no coherent national policy for the social and educational protection of children, either within the family or outside it. A number of initiatives based on the Convention on the Rights of the Child are underway; these should focus on the creation of such a coherent national policy, rather than on worthwhile but separate project objectives.

Street children

As more young people and families drift into cities in search of work, a combination of low-income levels, poor housing, high divorce rates and problems such as domestic violence and alcoholism sometimes leads to children and adolescents having to find their living in the streets. The number of street children in Latvia is still relatively small, although the problem is widely reported in the press and on television.

Not surprisingly, it is an urban rather than a rural phenomenon: the anonymity of urban street life offers an easier escape from the pressures of home and school. It also appeals more to boys than to girls, with boys outnumbering girls by about 3:1. A survey done in Riga in late 1997 found Latvian-speaking and Russian-speaking children about evenly represented. Their ages range from 5 to 15 with an average age of 11. They often live in groups of about 8-10 children, with strong internal hierarchies defined by age and physical strength. Most widely represented (45% of the total) was the 9-11 age group, with 12-15 year olds a close second at 40%. Most of the children were from Riga itself, but about 10% had come to the city from elsewhere in Latvia. A majority came from broken families, and a small but increasing number were runaways from orphanages or other institutions (17.6% in 1996, up from 14.3% in 1991). Most children in the survey (68%) said their families knew where they were; indeed 74% reported that they return home at night, while the others sleep in bus shelters, railway stations or in the city markets where they can get some food or money by begging. Most are adept at eluding the police, and most report enjoying life in the streets more than life at home although they still rely on their families for shelter and for an occasional change of clothes.[3] The team gained the impression that, although these children do not have the advantage of a stable family life, many of them have chosen life in the street rather than being forced into it in order to survive.

As for school attendance, only 23% of street children in the Riga survey said they did not attend school at all; the others said they did attend, although many were at least one year behind their age group. Several children reported that they did not like to go to school because teachers and the other children made fun of them or did not accept them. Because these children still have links with school, family and other social networks, the team believes that outreach programmes could be started in selected urban schools, perhaps providing an open learning centre with staff trained to work with socially marginalised or "problem" children. The OECD team understands that these issues are recognised by the MoES and the City of Riga, and that actions are being taken to address the problems within the framework of the Law on Education and Law on General Education.

At present, the only programme the team encountered was the City of Riga Prophylactic Centre for Minors Left Without Supervision (Rīgas pilsētas Galvenās policijas pārvaldes Kārtības policijas Nepilngadīgo profilakses centrs), a closed institution operated by the Ministry of the Interior, which can accept up to 50 children between the ages of 3-16. Minors found in the streets at night (mostly 11-13 year olds) can be detained there for temporary shelter for up to 60 or 90 days depending on the child's circumstances. However, because of a lack of protective legislation and follow-up social care, the Centre is a "revolving door" for some youngsters most at risk of falling foul of the law. No education is offered at the Centre; it is essentially a detention centre operated by the police, with some support from psychologists. There have been some proposals to set up a special school for street children as "potential delinquents", but the team believes that a more community-based approach – such as drop-in, open-learning centres perhaps supported by Child Hope, Save the Children and other NGOs as well as municipal authorities – would be preferable.

Dropout and unemployment

Some children may drift into street life for want of more productive things to do. Latvia has an excellent retention rate after the end of compulsory schooling (only about 6% of children do not continue into some kind of secondary education), but this still represents a significant number of young job seekers without experience or qualifications. In fact the percentage of job seekers in the 15-19 age group is 6.2 and 15.3% for 20-24 year olds[4]. The most promising strategy here would be to ensure that youngsters leaving the school system at age 15 have access to continuing education. The same concern applies to the high percentage of students who drop out of secondary education after their first year (for example, more than 50% of students who drop out from VET schools in 1997 was first year students).

The positive link between "children not attending school" and "street children" is clear from recent research[5]. School avoidance among street children is very high, and is cited by many children themselves as one of the main reasons why they left home. Lack of school success, finding the curriculum too difficult, hostility from pupils and teachers, boredom, and the cost of books and school clothes are the most frequently mentioned factors. Also, few schools are now able to offer the kind of after-school activities, sports and clubs that could attract at-risk youngsters to school life and that were part of complementary education under the previous system.

Due to the lack of reliable registers, there is no clear information about the numbers of children of compulsory school age who are not attending school. The best available estimate is provided by the campaign *Tevi gaida Skola* ("The School is Waiting for You", October 1997) which found approx. 3 500 children between the ages of 7 and 18 who did not attend school and did not complete primary education. In Latvia's present employment situation, these youngsters are unlikely to find legitimate jobs.

The team supports the type of youth interest programmes (clubs, activities, competitions, and festivals) now organised by the MoES's Division of Out-of-School Programmes, and would recommend expanding the budget for these programmes. In addition, collaboration with NGOs such as the Latvian Adult Education Association and with the 27 Adult Education Centres now operating throughout Latvia should help provide out-of-school youngsters with a range of formal and informal education, vocational education, and higher education opportunities leading to some form of marketable qualification. For example, extending Latvian-language courses to non-Latvian speaking youngsters would help prevent their long-term exclusion from the job market.

Exceptional children: special needs education in Latvia

Policy

Latvia's strong record of providing educational opportunities for all mem-bers of the community provides a positive starting point for a discussion of its policies on special needs education. Taken in a broad sense, "special needs" includes not only children with physical or mental disabilities but children with developmental, behavioural or serious social problems – that is, children of normal intelligence and physical ability who nevertheless need special help in order to achieve. In Latvia, special needs education is defined as "general edu-cation with emphasis on practical and vocational skills for children with mental and physical handicaps as well as psycho-neurological and serious somatic diseases".[6]

As is clear from this definition, the Soviet science of "defectology" still deeply affects the notion of education for exceptional children throughout the former Soviet Union. Its main interpretation – although not its initial, holistic intention – is medical, aimed at diagnosing and then correcting or compensa-ting for the "defect". Up to the 1950s, special education was almost exclusively provided at facilities for deaf, blind, or mentally retarded children; behavioural and developmental problems were ignored until the 1970s, and even then were approached in the same medical, "corrective" way, addressing the "defect" rather than the child.

Policy on special needs education in Latvia, as in so many former commu-nist countries, is still largely based on a traditional, collectivist approach emphasising the role of the state. Its main features are (1) emphasis on institutional, publicly financed care rather than on family-based support; (2) little attention paid to other than medically diagnosed mental, physical or developmental handicaps; (3) large, closed or semi-closed institutions (orphanages, special boarding schools), with on average more than 100 child-ren each.

Other problems are the fragmentation of responsibility among several Ministries (*e.g.* Welfare, Health, Education) and lack of co-ordination. Indeed the design of the current system does not encourage co-ordination and supervision of effort; Ministries compete to secure larger roles and larger financial allocations. Departmental interests inhibit information sharing and collaboration, resulting in inflated administrative costs, lack of transpa-rency, and lack of reliable data about who is being served, and by whom.

129

Placement and provision

The proportion of children placed in institutions is relatively high by international standards. Yet there are still categories of children for whom special provision does not exist. Examples include children with common learning disabilities such as dyslexia or attention deficit disorder; or psychological disorders such as "non-organic failure to thrive", affective disorders, and other syndromes identified in recent years and covered in international classifications of special needs such as those used by the World Health Organisation.

At Ministry level, there is a state Pedagogical Medical Commission (PMPC) (*Valst pedagogiski mediciniska komisija*) with nine staff and a small budget (approx. 4 000 lats/year) and a programme aimed at improving integration of special needs children into regular schools. Each rajon and each major city has its own PMPC, financed from the rajon or city budget. These PMPCs are the diagnostic authorities responsible for the placement – subject to parents' consent – of children in special educational programmes or institutions.

A typical PMPC consists of two to five members, who evaluate every child referred to them. Diagnoses tend to be made on the basis of short sporadic contacts between evaluators and a child, instead of long-term observations; tests and diagnostic equipment are often outdated. The consequences for the (already vulnerable) child, however, can be severe. The following problems need particular attention, especially for institutionalised children:

- Early "labelling" of children on the basis of superficial evidence, damaging a child's self-esteem as well as his/her long-term chances for educational success, a job, or any kind of social acceptance.

- Misdiagnoses or vague diagnoses that do not allow the development of suitable individual educational programmes, or place the child in "corrective" programmes of doubtful value.

- Over-diagnosis of conditions that do not, internationally, warrant special education or institutional placement. An obvious example of this is the extraordinary emphasis on "scoliosis" (curvature of the spine), which even in some regular schools is said to affect 50% of children. The team visited several general schools and kindergartens employing full-time, qualified doctors, physiotherapists and nursing staff to work with these "scoliosis" children; one suburban state-funded pre-school had a heated swimming pool where a group of eight children were supervised by two instructors and a qualified nurse. Given the under-funding and severe financial constraints under which the Latvian education system operates, efficient use of resources is surely essential. Equipment and staff that deliver services of marginal therapeutic or educational value, however attractive, should be reconsidered.

- Disincentives built into the public care system, which encourage institutions to have as many "labelled" children as possible, since this increases budget allocations, creates jobs (*e.g.* speech therapists, masseurs and physiotherapists, nursing staff etc.), and may be used to justify low pupil-teacher ratios.

Mainstreaming

While there is general support for the idea of "mainstreaming" special needs children as much as possible by integrating them into regular schools, the team heard that Latvia does not, at present, wish to adopt this as a general policy. Wide professional and public discussion on this issue, culminating in an international conference held in Riga in the autumn of 1998, came to the view that "It is no good sowing seeds in unprepared ground": teachers, schools, and communities are not yet ready. In a 1998 survey, only 16% of teachers said they would be prepared to accept special needs children; 21% said they would, if they could receive special help; but overall only 9% agreed that children with special needs should, preferably, be educated in regular schools. Very few schools at present have wheelchair access or suitable toilet facilities.

More seriously, poor parents and those in rural areas cannot provide the sort of medical support that is now available in Latvia's network of special institutions. It would therefore not be in the interests of children and their families to take large numbers of them out of institutionalised care. The team heard that an estimated two-thirds of children now in special institutions come from poor families: medical help at home is simply not an option, although "half of the special needs children now in institutions could go home if medical services were available". It was also said that the majority of institutionalised children need a "home" as well as specialised care; many families are unable to provide adequate clothing and nutrition, and in rural areas transport between home and school (especially for handicapped children) is not available.

For the time being, therefore, MoES policy is to maintain a strong institutional network while proceeding with caution towards greater integration into general schools. One innovative approach favoured by the MoES is to convert special needs schools into general schools: compared with the high cost of equipping and training a general school to accommodate special needs children,

131

it may be more efficient to use existing special-needs facilities and staff for general use. It may not be feasible to turn all schools into "mainstream" schools, but some could become "development schools" to serve as models and disseminate good integration practice. At the time of the team's visit, five such "development" schools were already in operation; two in Riga, and three regional schools – one in Kurzeme and two in Vidzeme.

Numbers

Reliable data on the numbers of children formally in special education during the Soviet period are scarce. Even scarcer are any data on special needs children who, during those years, fell through the educational net altogether, who struggled and failed in regular schools where they were expected to cope with regular curricula. Some children never went to school at all, especially in rural areas where "going to school" was hard enough for ordinary children. Since 1991, changes are evident in both quantity and quality of special needs education in Latvia. Figures show a rapid increase in the numbers of children identified as having special needs (from 6 200 in 1971 to nearly 10 000 in 1997). Numbers are still rising, partly because the definition of "special needs" is now broader, and partly because children previously considered uneducable are now gradually being included in the system. Only about 0.5% of compulsory school age children are now not in school due to disability.

Table 9. **Special Needs Children**
1998 and 1999

Description	1998	1999	Comments
Total number of children with special needs (all types, including behavioural problems)	14 500	15 500	Nearly 7% increase
Of these, children needing continual medical care (*e.g.* children with TB, multiple handicaps etc.)	9 943	10 022	Slight increase
State budget for Special Needs of all types	16 441 000 lats	16 221 000 lats	Slight decrease. This amount is said to cover only two-thirds of what SN schools need
Number of institutions	63	64	43 of these are for mentally handicapped children

Source: Ministry of Education and Science, Riga, 1999.

The continuing rise in numbers, as well as greater sensitivity to the vulnerable status of children in less-stable, post-communist societies, have stimulated discussion among Latvian educators about the relation between special and "regular" education, the notion of "mainstreaming", and the merits of separate, specialised provision. They are discussing the way in which "defectology" still affects the concept and organisation of special education in Latvia. Although the educational rights of special needs children are protected by Latvian law as well as by the UN Convention on the Rights of the Child, many schools, teachers, and members of the public are unsympathetic to the integration of these children in regular classrooms. The team supports recent efforts to raise teacher and public awareness, but more is needed to protect disadvantaged children's educational rights, especially as schooling becomes more selective and municipalities struggle to meet basic financial obligations.

Educational programmes

Where children are of normal intellect but handicapped in other ways (*e.g.* physically), state standards, curricula and examinations apply. Differentiated curricula for special needs children have been under development for three years with wide consultation; where possible, students themselves have been involved in their development. When a child cannot cope with these, special programmes are designed without compulsory components, standard tests, or centrally marked examinations. The emphasis is on "making it possible for the child to develop and live usefully in society".

"Living usefully" will require at least some opportunity for special needs youngsters to become self-sufficient. Unfortunately, vocational schools have thus far been reluctant to provide special vocational training. In 1993/94, the Ministry moved to provide special programmes in vocational education and Grade ten classes, but only if the receiving school has the necessary resources, and only if there are prospects of employment for at least 50% of the special needs children at the end of their training. Given the levels of unemployment in the country, these provisos give unwilling vocational schools a convenient excuse; nevertheless, more vocational schools are now accepting special-needs youngsters because birth rates and enrolment rates are falling, and many vocational schools are overstaffed for the numbers of students they attract.

Financing

1. The quality of care and education received by special needs children is of course dependent on adequate and reliable funding: children's needs do not change when GDP falls, but they are vulnerable when budgets have to be cut.

Latvian special needs education is financed from the state budget as determined by the Cabinet of Ministers. The state guarantees provision for individuals with mental, physical and developmental disorders, and their right to receive general and vocational education and to participate in the work force. Municipalities are obliged to provide a minimum level of assistance; law guarantees this. They receive earmarked subsidies from the state budget to support special boarding schools, salaries of staff, transport costs and other types of expenditure. However, the team heard that budget allocations cover only two-thirds of actual need. There are ways in which special needs institutions can generate additional income; some, for example, grow crops like potatoes that can either be used by the institution itself or sold for profit, but others find it hard to make ends meet.

2. Moreover, there is concern among special-needs professionals that state subsidies are targeted on institutions and not on children. With an increasing number of children being integrated into regular schools (approximately 8 000 in 1998), there is a need to ensure that special assistance reaches every child entitled to it, whether he/she is in a "special-purpose" institution or not. Clauses 60-62 of the Law on General Education should be amended to make this clear.

Recommendations to counter social exclusion

1. Keeping in mind the question, "Who is being served?" radically reconsider the issue of co-ordination, responsibility, and accountability among different levels and branches of government, especially in relation to funding mechanisms for poverty relief and social support.

2. Approach rural development issues such as the closure of small rural schools or agricultural schools with full attention to the effects of such closures on the social fabric of communities and on the real-life educational prospects of children.

3. Co-ordinate the work of various Ministries and municipalities to create the kind of unified "child register" that provides a firm basis for its key policy and resource decisions. At present, data gathered under separate sets of regulations are contradictory and inadequate. Social welfare registers of children in at-risk families could also be useful. Ensure that legislation is in line with the UN Convention on the Rights of the Child, which has been ratified by Latvia.

4. Develop a coherent national policy for the social and educational protection of children, both within the family and outside it. Various initiatives based on the Convention on the Rights of the Child are underway; these should

focus on the creation of such a coherent national policy, rather than on worth-while but separate project objectives.

5. Instead of treating street children as actual or potential delinquents and dealing with them mostly through Minors Affairs Inspection units (*Nepilngadigo lietu inspekcija*) and the state and municipal police, adopt more community-based approaches. Examples include drop-in, open-learning centres, perhaps suppor-ted by Child Hope, Save the Children and other NGOs as well as municipal authorities. Children should be helped to obtain information about social assistance and educational opportunities suitable to them.

6. Support and expand the youth interest programmes (clubs, activities, competitions, and festivals) now organised by the MoES's Department of Adult and Continuing Education, and increase their share of the Department's budget. Work with the 27 municipally-funded Adult Education Centres now operating throughout Latvia; also involve NGOs such as the Latvian Adult Education Association to provide out-of-school youngsters with a range of formal and infor-mal education, Latvian language courses, vocational education and higher edu-cation opportunities leading to a marketable qualification.

Recommendations regarding special needs children

1. Ensure that money flows to every child identified as having special needs, wherever that child may be at home, in a regular school, or in a special-pur-pose educational institution, and clarify the law to that effect.

2. Continue the measured approach towards "mainstreaming", taking care not to jeopardise the interests of children in poor families and rural areas where medical support to families is not available on a daily basis. In prac-tice, this means maintaining institutional care levels while laying the groundwork for greater integration.

3. Strengthen the support to families, where possible. In Latvia, where s-ociety still does not easily accept special needs children and has been reluctant to integrate them into the community, this is a major challenge. Municipalities might introduce parental support programmes connected with day "clubs" or support units for disabled children living with their families, perhaps similar to the Social Rehabilitation Centres for Handicapped Children that have been set up in Lithuania. There is a great deal of international experience that could be drawn upon; the Ministry already has active links with Austria and Sweden that could be used for such work.

4. Develop alternative forms of institutional care, bringing living conditions as close as possible to those in families. Large institutions within which children receive their schooling as well as their full-time care tend to isolate youngsters from their communities. Smaller, mixed-age groups of children living with house parents and attending local schools allow them to mix more easily with other children. Children's village, foster care, and small family-type models have been tried in other countries, and can be low-cost and partially self-sustaining.

5. Improve data collection, management, and co-ordination among different agencies providing care. A coherent database is necessary for targeted use of scarce resources. Perhaps bringing all institutionalised childcare under a single governing authority would simplify the unnecessarily complex structure and make it more transparent.

6. Modernise the basis on which children are identified, diagnosed, and placed in special needs programmes. In particular, it is important to introduce all PMPCs (*Valst pedagogiski mediciniska komisija*) to modern diagnostic standards, techniques and equipment to reduce the risks of mis-diagnosis.

Notes

1.   Ministry of Welfare, Social Report 1998, p. 11.

2.   UNICEF, Children at Risk in Central and Eastern Europe: Perils and Promises. Regional Monitoring Report No. 4, UNICEF International Child Development Centre, Florence, 1997, p. 152. Occasional social assistance was rendered in 406 cases per 10 000 population in 1992, rising to more than 5 500 cases per 10 000 population by 1995.

3.   Project "Child in the Street", Higher School for Social Work and Social Pedagogy Attistiba and the Centre for Criminological research. Riga: 1997, pp. 21 et seq.

4.   Academic Information Centre – Latvian National Observatory. From materials of national report on the modernisation of VET System in Latvia to European Training Foundation, 1999.

5.   Project 'Child in the Street', op.cit., pp. 51 et seq.

6.   Anna Dreimane, "Special Education in Latvia". Unpublished paper; Ministry of Education and Science, 1998, p. 3.

Chapter 6

Higher Education

Policy structure and governance

The Law on Education and the 1995 Law on Higher Education Establishments provide these institutions with substantial autonomy from the state. Autonomy encompasses the authority to establish the content and forms of study, supplementary conditions for admission of students, basic directions of scientific and research work, and the organisational and administrative structure. Within limits established by the Cabinet of Ministers, institutions have autonomy in hiring of personnel and setting their compensation rates. Institutions are legal entities and are largely self-governing within the provisions established by each institution's constitution (*Satversme*). The *Satversme* of universities must be approved by the *Saeima*, while the constitutions of other higher education institutions are approved by the Cabinet of Ministers.

With the constraints imposed by institutional autonomy, the MoES has formal authority to implement the Law on Higher Education Establishments, and the Minister represents the interests of higher education before the Cabinet of Ministers and the *Saeima*. The MoES is responsible for licensing of institutions and for carrying out the accreditation process according to regulations established by the Cabinet of Ministers. A decision to reorganise or close an institution must be taken by the Cabinet of Ministers, based on a recommendation of the MoES and a study by the Council on Higher Education. Several ministries (Agriculture, Culture, Internal Affairs, Defence and Welfare) in addition to the MoES continue to serve as founders of state higher education establishments. These ministries are responsible for supervision, professional curricula, and financing of the institutions within their jurisdiction, but the MoES is responsible for accreditation of all study programmes and institutions.

Rectors of higher education establishments are elected according to the *Satversme* for a five-year term and may not serve more than two terms. The election of rectors must be approved by the Cabinet of Ministers on the recommendation of the MoES. Dismissal of a rector is the responsibility of the Cabinet of Ministers. The Council of Rectors is responsible for promoting co-ordination and co-operation among higher education establishments and advising the MoES and Cabinet of Ministers. The Council of Rectors is responsible for deciding on joint study programmes, evaluating draft laws, and drafting proposals for distribution of state budgetary resources among higher education institutions.

The Council on Higher Education is an independent institution that develops national strategy in higher education, strengthens co-operation, oversees the quality, and prepares the ground for decisions in issues related to higher education. It consists of nine members; besides higher education and student representatives, members are drawn from the Academy of Sciences, the Council of Creative Unions, Association of Leaders of Education, the Union of Doctors, and the Chamber of Commerce and Industry. The Minister of Education and Science is an ex-officio member with voting rights. The *Saeima*, on the proposal of the Minister of Education and Science, confirms membership of the Council. Among its basic responsibilities, the most prominent are the accreditation of higher education institutions and the forecasting of the number of budget-students in each branch. The Council also serves in an advisory capacity to the Minister of Education and Science and to the higher education department of the MoES. The Chairman and deputy are elected; the Chairman serves as the executive of the Council. A representative of the MoES participates in meetings as a "standing advisor".[1]

Among the functions of the Council on Higher Education are to:

- Formulate a national concept for the development of higher education and higher education establishments;

- Formulate long-term plans and proposals for development of education and research within the system of higher education;

- Develop proposals to raise the quality of research activities and study programmes and the qualifications of the staff;

- Forecast the number of students necessary for the country in general and work out proposals regarding the numbers of students financed from the state budget in each branch;

- Develop proposals for changes in the structure of higher education establishments;

- Develop proposals for the number of professors and other issues;

- Develop programmes on improvement of higher education and the payment of tuition fees;

- Advise the Cabinet of Ministers on the proposed state budget for higher education;

- Make decisions on accreditation of institutions and submit them for approval by the MoES; and

- Prepare programmes for integrating science and higher education, and implement them within the limits of the Council's competence.

Institutions of higher education

Latvian institutions of higher education are divided into universities, establishments for professionals, other higher education establishments. Traditional state institutions offer at least three levels of degrees, while institutions that do not have university status and newly established private institutions usually specialise in one or more fields and often grant degrees only below doctoral level. Universities are defined as institutions that cover one or several major scientific fields, and are entitled to confer degrees up to the doctoral degree Higher expectations are established for universities with respect to research and the integration of research and teaching. As indicated above, university constitutions (*Satversme*) must be approved by the *Saeima*. The accreditation process for universities must involve international representatives. According to a decision of the Latvian Council of Higher Education, there are six state institutions with university status (University of Latvia, Riga Technical University with Riga Business Institute, Latvia University of Agriculture, Medical Academy of Latvia, and Daugavpils Pedagogical University).

There are 14 other institutions of higher education, which have no university status and are in principle specialised in one or a small number of disciplines. Six of these grant up to the first doctoral degree or doktors, usually internationally equated with a Ph.D. (the Latvian Academy of Music, the Latvian Academy of Arts, the Latvian Academy of Culture, the Liepâja Pedagogical Academy, the Latvian Academy of Sports Education, and the Police Academy of Latvia). Degrees below doctoral level are granted by another eight institutions (the Latvian Maritime Academy, the National Academy of Defence of the Republic of Latvia, Rēzekne Higher Education Institution, Riga Higher School of Pedagogy and School Management, the Stockholm School of Economics in Riga, the Banking College of Higher Education, Vidzeme College of Higher Education, and Ventspils College). The last two institutions have been established in the academic year 1996/1997 and are still at an early stage of development.

In recent years, a number of private institutions have been established. According to law, these institutions can be divided into licensed and accredited private institutions. If an institution of higher education is established by a legal entity, that entity must be founded by the Cabinet of Ministers on the basis of an application by MoES. They must be licensed by the MoES in accordance with regulations of the Cabinet of Ministers. Licensed institutions and their study programmes may then be accredited. At the time of the review, there were five accredited institutions running accredited study programmes (Higher School of Social Work and Social Pedagogic "Attîstîba", Business School Turîba, Riga International College of Economics and Business Administration, Business Institute RIMPAK Livonia, and the Baltic Russian Institute). Institutions are accredited on the basis of a systematic quality assessment procedure. Accreditation allows an institution to grant diplomas and degrees that are recognised by the state. Licensed private institutions are those that have not yet undergone this accreditation procedure, but have been granted a license to operate based on a preliminary examination of their curricula and facilities. Eight licensed institutions – the International Institute of Practical Psychology, the Institute of Social Technologies, the Riga Humanitarian Institute, the Riga Institute of Aeronavigation, the Latvian Evangelic Christian Academy, the College of Information Systems Management, the College of Economics and Culture, and the College of Psychology – exist legally and are working to meet accreditation criteria. The OECD team heard reports there are, however, some other private institutions which operate without a license and consequently without any state oversight in contradiction to the Law on Higher Education Establishments. Students enrolled in these institutions – and to some extent in any institution that has been licensed but not accredited – have no guarantee that their diplomas and degrees will be recognised by the state.

The 1995 Law on Higher Education Establishments authorises "colleges" under the supervision of higher education establishments to provide professional education studies of less than four years. The law makes clear, however, that these studies are not to be considered "higher education". Universities and academies therefore provide both academic and professional (vocational) study programmes. Judging by their content, it is not always clear why some courses are considered academic rather than professional. Financial difficulties often oblige universities and academies to organise courses that are distinctly community-focused, but irrelevant to any academic discipline. Moreover, in other countries, many of these courses would be part of post-secondary (non-university) vocationally oriented systems. This underscores the need to develop a genuine non-university higher education sector for Latvia, comparable to *Ammattikorkeakoulu* in Finland, *Fachhochschulen* in Germany, *Hoger Beroeps Onderwijs* (HBO) in the Netherlands, or *Hogescholen* in Flanders (Belgium). The recently enacted (June 1999) Law on Vocational and Professional Education formally authorises this level of education for the first time in Latvia.

Students

Enrolment trends

Student enrolments in higher education have increased sharply in recent years after a decline following re-establishment of independence. Enrolments dropped from more than 45 000 in 1990 to 33 000 in 1993. By 1995/96, enrolments had increased to 46 153, including 2 936 in private establishments. Enrolments increased to 76 653 by 1998/99 (a 66% increase), including 8 628 in private institutions.[2] The students themselves have financed much of this enrolment increase. Enrolments financed by the state budget increased from 30 181 in 1995/96 to 32 763 in 1998/99, a 7.9% increase. Over the same period, the number of fee-paying students increased from 15 972 to 43 890, a 175% increase. The proportion of fee-paying enrolments in state-owned institutions increased from 30.16% in 1995/96 to 52.22% in 1998/99.[3] Obviously, this increase in student enrolments is caused primarily by a dramatic change in the labour market, but it also reflects a change in values. As in other countries of the region, entrance into higher education provides an outlet to an important segment of the population – young people unable to find employment. However, the rise in numbers reflects more than an "escape route" from unemployment; it is also evident that the educational aspirations and career ambitions of the population have risen considerably in Latvia's new social and political circumstances. A higher education degree gives better possibilities for employment, but it is also a better preparation to participate actively in society, in professional as well as in individual life. Thus, the development of higher education perhaps represents one of the most dramatic and positive ways for young people to change their personal behaviour after the collapse of the planned economy and during the country's difficult transformation into a market economy. Today, nearly 40% of 19-23 year olds take part in some form of tertiary education.[4]

There are also a growing number of students (34%) enrolling less than full time, most of whom are correspondence students.[5] Part-time, correspondence and extramural studies provide opportunities for older, "second chance" students and to those who want to complete their higher education degree and improve their position in the labour market.

Changes in students by fields of study

In Latvia, as in other former communist countries, the main field of study was engineering (50% in the former USSR), while the proportion of students in the social sciences was less than 10%. Global economic changes contributed most to the rapid and dramatic fall in the proportion of students choosing engineering in the first half of the 1990s. In 1998 it reached a "normal" level (16%), which is average for industrialised countries, although still much higher than in the US and Canada (where it is approximately 9%). The other side of this process was an enormous increase in social sciences entrants; here, the proportion reached 44% of all students by 1998, well above average rates in industrialised countries. Changes are seen also in other fields. The proportion of students in agricultural (10.2% in 1992, 3.2% in 1998) and natural sciences (7.1% in 1992, 3.8% in 1998) as well as in health protection (6.2% in 1992, 1.7% in 1998) decreased sharply. The already high rate of students in teacher education increased still further (14% in 1992, 17.4% in 1998) despite the expected sharp drop in school cohorts.[6] Whether these changes were spontaneous or the result of deliberate planning, a post-Soviet restructuring of the studies offered in higher education was inevitable. However, they also raise some serious questions. Reduction of student numbers in engineering clearly poses a threat to an old – and traditionally highly esteemed – discipline associated with high performance. Premises, equipment and teachers could not be simply removed or used in another discipline; therefore the reduction brought financial problems to old institutions. The decrease in students was also at least partially a result of various "transitional" problems, and even a certain mass psychology ("Nobody studies engineering").

An additional problem is caused by the fact that a decrease in student numbers usually also means a decrease in students with top academic results. However, the political support for engineering remains strong and engineering as a discipline will survive, or at least its highest-quality part. Market forces will best equalise supply and demand in this specific field, but attention should be drawn to institutions with both a high reputation and an established tradition, and they should not merely be left to an uncertain destiny. Once stabilised, the national economy will again need experts in this field; probably in a much smaller proportion than in the past, but of the same or higher quality. Therefore, the question is not how to preserve the study of engineering, but how to adapt it – including its content – to new economic, social and cultural realities.

The social sciences, on the other hand, encounter completely opposite problems. The abrupt increase of interest in this field was based mainly on the fact that the new economic circumstances give much more scope and better career prospects to specialists in economics, law, business, languages, etc., and also that there were practically no people with such qualifications among previous university graduates. Of course, a certain dose of transitional illusion ("a businessman with a mobile phone") played a part, but it is evident that the social sciences will continue to absorb resources for some time to come. However, even here, facilities, equipment, and teachers could not be simply brought from elsewhere; rapid development therefore raises questions of quality. This potential danger was quickly recognised in Latvia, and the team considers that the education system, at the right time, protected the quality of higher education by introducing a special accreditation procedure.

Changes in the birth rate and the demand for higher education

The natural population increase in Latvia was constant over the post-war period. In an average age cohort of that time, there were 31 000 to 36 000 children. In the late 1970s and first half of the 1980s, a huge increase was evident, with a maximum of 42 000 born in 1986. After this time, however, the country has encountered a rapid decrease in its birth rate; in 1996, only 21 000 children were born, half of the 1986 cohort. The decrease in the birth rate has already reached basic education, and higher education will be affected after 2005. It should not be overlooked that higher education today is besieged by the large cohorts of the first half of the 1980s, and that in five or ten years the situation will be completely different. Such exceptional turbulence in demography is a warning signal, and demands special measures to strengthen national education and to prevent undesirable effects. At the same time, experience in other countries shows that the educational aspirations of young people rise faster than their numbers. Consequently, although the cohorts of students reaching the end of secondary education may be smaller, more of them will expect to continue into some form of tertiary education. The development of a non-university "colleges" as authorised by the Law on Vocational Education and Training will be important to respond to these changing expectations and needs.

Financing

In the past, higher education was free of charge, but the places available were strictly planned and limited. The scarcity of budget resources, and the ever-increasing number of candidates, have produced an unusual combination of state-supported and fee-paying students. The Law on Higher Education Establishments stipulates that the state budget for financing higher education establishments is to come from several sources. These include basic financing for the "optimum number of lists of study programmes and the number of students covering resources to pay for public utilities, taxes, infrastructure maintenance, purchase of equipment and inventory, research and artistic creativity as well as salaries for the staff". The state budget may also provide other funding for specialised state purposes, for science, and for the tuition and fees for students receiving state-financed loans.[7] The Law also authorises special state loans from a study fund established by the Cabinet of Ministers.

The state budget for higher education increased from 20.3 million lats in 1995 to 25.6 million lats in 1998, or by 26%. During the same period, institutional funding from paid services (student fees) increased from 3.9 lats to 8.4 lats, or by 115%. The total funding as a percentage of Gross Domestic Product (GDP) remained essentially constant.

Table 10. **Financing Higher Education**
1995 to 1998 (millions of lats)

Year	State Budget*	Paid Services	Total	% of GDP
1995	20.3	3.9 (19.2%)	24.2	1.18
1996	23.1	3.6 (15.6%)	26.7	0.98
1997	23.4	6.6 (27.8%)	30.0	0.98
1998	25.6	8.4 (32.8%)	34.0	1.02

Note: * Subsidy of general incomes, including the means granted for investments
Source: Republic of Latvia, Council on Higher Education, The National Concept of the Development of Higher Education and the Institutions of Higher Education of the Republic of Latvia, Riga 1998, p. 13.

The Council on Higher Education is legally responsible for ascertaining the number of students financed by the state budget in each establishment. The Government formally approves this number based on a recommendation from the MoES. Students may either be in fully or partially state-funded (budget) places. (That is, fee-paying students may pay either full or partial fees.) The institutions establish the level of student fees. In spite of the Council's formal role in determining state budget places, it is a new institution and at the time of the OECD review it had not been able to affect significantly the historic distribution among major sectors. Consequently, there were significant variations among institutions in the number of state-budget students. These variations also reflect differences in student demand: students are willing to pay for places at the more popular institutions and disciplines. At the main national institution – the University of Latvia, with a total of 22 758 students – there are only 30.9% state-budget students, while at Riga Technical University 78% are state-budget students. Some institutions of a special national interest that are supervised by ministries other than the MoES have very high rates of budget students. These include the National Academy of Defence of the Republic of Latvia (100%), the Latvian Academy of Music (98.5%), the Latvian Maritime Academy (94.6%), and the Police Academy of Latvia (86.7%). In addition to the continuation of historic patterns of budget and non-budget students, state financing policy currently does not reflect differences in costs among disciplines. Since 1998 the Cabinet of Ministers regulations on financing normatives of higher education establishements stipulate differentiated national budget's financing for various study programmes.

Issues identified in the course of the review

Access to higher education and the issue of fairness

The review team is aware that, in many countries, the circumstances of the social transition have made the issue of access to higher education extremely complex. This is the case in Latvia as well. On the positive side, higher education is no longer a centrally planned system intended for a very small proportion of the population, but has opened up to provide more individuals with an opportunity to develop abilities and skills and attain social promotion. Today, the most numerous age cohorts – those born during the first half of the 1980s – are entering Latvian higher education. Social circumstances more than ever stimulate youngsters to continue their study at tertiary level. Moreover – in relative as well as absolute figures – there are more who finish an adequate secondary school and fulfil the entrance conditions to enrol at a higher education institution. The expansion of higher education during the period of social transition is of vital importance for the future of all newly independent societies, including Latvia.

On the less positive side, however, it is obvious that the actual conditions in which expansion must take place are more severe than ever. Two issues are of particular concern with respect to access and fairness. These are the increasing costs being borne by students through fees, and the continuing complexities of the processes for entering higher education.

Student financing

As discussed earlier, the number of fee-paying students increased by 175% from 1995/96 to 1998/99, with the result that these students now constitute more than 50% of enrolments. The review team recognises that the distinction bet-

147

ween budget and non-budget students is a feature of the post-Soviet transitional period. The budget students are a legacy of the former planned system, while the non-budget ones represent a spontaneous reaction of a market economy still in its early stages; the situation is determined also by limited budget resources. The team is concerned that it may produce serious problems with respect to issues of fairness and open access to higher education. There is clearly a need for a national policy that targets limited state budgetary resources on the disciplines and professions most important to the future of the nation. It is also important to ensure that students from all social and economic circumstances and from both rural and urban areas can afford to gain access to those disciplines and professions.

The OECD review team was encouraged by indications that Latvia was concerned about these issues and that changes in policies for financing of higher education were under consideration. Regulations on student loans (credits) of the Cabinet of Ministers came into effect on June 15, 1997. At the time of the review in February 1999, a new plan for implementing student loans (credits) had been completed for consideration by the Cabinet of Ministers. This plan came into effect on March 9, 1999, through Regulation 86 of the Cabinet of Ministers. In addition to providing financing assistance to students, Latvia must also address underlying questions about how to finance a system that is rapidly moving from an élite to a mass higher education system. OECD countries throughout the world are debating issues about the appropriate role of student fees as their higher education systems make this transition. Latvia has been moving toward a system financed heavily by student fees not because of deliberate policy choice but because of severe economic conditions. It is now important that the national develop a financing policy framework for the future.

Process for gaining entrance

As indicated earlier in this chapter, student numbers have more than doubled in the past six years. The students' demand now is far greater than the institutions' supply; therefore, students – but also institutions – find themselves in a competitive situation. There is no centralised application procedure, and students, to secure a place, have to apply to more than one institution and wait for the outcome of multiple selection procedures. At the same time, institutions have more applicants but they cannot be sure that all students who succeed in the selection procedure will actually enrol, as they might be admitted to other institutions as well.

The principle of granting educational opportunities to individuals according to their merits and demands has two main aspects. First, prospective students are entitled to a transparent system of application and admission; second, they should be able to follow the most direct route to realisation of their study intentions, choices and wishes. Transparency is closely related to fairness (e.g. avoiding privileges of any kind); while the realisation of individual intentions is usually an excellent predictor of study success. However, under the present conditions, candidates enter a complicated system of entrance examinations and selection which is neither transparent nor fair, and insufficiently sensitive to the reasons underlying differences in student performance. An individual's success or failure in a selection procedure of this type – i.e. the combination of a study intention with its financial consequences in the shape of a state-granted or fee-paying place – is not a precisely measured result of that individual's abilities and skills. It is much more influenced by his or her former education, background, social and cultural environment, and economic means. The selection procedures that are now used independently by each higher education institution can only work against individuals from less advantaged backgrounds.

The review team has therefore paid special attention to the connection between secondary and tertiary education (see Chapter), and to the project led by the MoES to establish a national examination at the end of secondary education. Such a project should receive full support. It is important not only as an instrument to improve secondary education but also as an instrument to make the performance of different schools and achievements of students more comparable and to reduce failure to a certain degree. It is important also from the point of view of equity. National examinations are closely related to national standards; they give clear evidence of performance, and can serve as an important tool for decision-makers in developing the educational system properly, reducing disadvantage, and giving equal opportunities to all students insofar as possible.

A reliable national examination system at the end of secondary will, in the team's view, also improve transparency and fairness in access to higher education. If it is accepted by higher education institutions as adequate for classification and selection purposes, it can in due course be extended to a national system for university admission, eliminating the need for separate entrance examinations at different institutions and relieving candidates of the pressures and uncertainty now associated with university admissions.

Quality assurance

Through the provisions of the Law on Higher Education Establishments and the work of the Council on Higher Education, Latvia has made significant progress in addressing issues of quality assurance in higher education. The OECD team is aware, however, that major challenges remain in fully implemen-

149

ting an effective quality assurance process for the whole system. The Law on Education and Law on Higher Education Establishments set forth the basic framework for quality assurance. According to this law, all state higher education establishments have been conditionally accredited until the end of 2001. A new accreditation process must be completed by that time. The MoES is responsible for licensing institutions, the basic requirement for all institutions, whether founded by the state or private entities (legal persons). The Law on Higher Education Establishments requires that all institutions and study programmes leading to state approved higher education credentials be accredited. The Cabinet of Ministers sets forth the regulations for accreditation. There are essentially two processes, one focused on the accreditation of institutions, and the other on the accreditation of study programmes. The institutional accreditation process includes an extensive application and a requirement for an institutional self-study. An evaluation team, including international representatives, reviews the self-study, makes a site visit, and submits its recommendations to the Council on Higher Education. The Council then makes a decision on accreditation that is adopted by the MoES. The Law on Higher Education Establishments also requires that each study programme be accredited every six years. Accrediting commissions are established to undertake the assessments and to make recommendations to the Council on Higher Education. These commissions are composed of experts from the disciplines and professions under review as well as representatives of the Academy of Sciences, the Chamber of Trade and Industry, and other public organisations. As in the case of the accreditation of institutions, the Council on Higher Education makes the final determination subject to approval of the MoES.[8]

Following establishment of the Higher Education Quality Assurance Centre in 1995, quality assessment began in 1996/97. Assessment of all institutions and study programmes is expected to be completed by 2002. The OECD team had an opportunity to examine the self-study documents from two institutions and to discuss the process with the institutions as well as the Council on Higher Education. The processes reflect the best practices of several OECD countries and, if fully implemented, will have a significant impact on quality and on the standing of Latvian institutions in the international community.

Colleges and non-university studies

As was stated earlier, Latvia took at important step in providing the legal basis for higher (non-university) vocational/professional education through the Law on Vocational and Training enacted in June 1999. The OECD team is concerned, however, that ambiguities remain regarding the mission of "colleges" in Latvia. The new institutions (higher professional education at the first level) authorised by the Law on Vocational and Training would function within the framework of that law and outside the policy framework for higher education. At the same time, the provisions of the Law on Higher Education Establishments (Article 25) authorising institutions to offer study programmes in "colleges" at the non-university level (level two of higher professional education) remain.

The experience of OECD countries underscores that non-university sectors should have strong "horizontal" relationships with employers, the labour market, and the economies of their regions. Their primary mission should be to prepare students to enter the labour market with a combination of strong academic and professional competence at a post-secondary level. If non-university sectors are too closely tied to higher education institutions – especially academic institutions with strong research missions – the "vertical" pressures of the university tend to dominate. The emphasis shifts from preparing students for the labour market, to preparing students for university entrance. The requirements for faculty appointments tend to emphasise advanced academic credentials and evidence of research productivity rather than strong teaching skills, links with the labour market, and skills to prepare students for professions.

All countries establishing new non-university sectors pass through a period in which the institutions are not well understood either by employers or by prospective students and their parents. In a period of a surplus of educated workers, many employers continue to use a higher education credential as a means to screen potential employees although the credential may have little relationship to the actual required skills. Recognising this tendency, parents and students see a university credential as the only path toward employment and increased social status. As the economy develops, however, both employers and students will increasing see the non-university sector as the key to preparation for employment as well as access to tertiary education.

A degree of separation between the developing colleges and university institutions is important. Yet, the policies that ensure smooth student transfer from one sector to another are equally important. Because of rapid changes in the labour market and the need for lifelong learning, many of these students will need to pursue further education and training – including a university degree. Therefore, students who complete college-level education should be able to enter a higher education institution or university with the minimum of complication and without the need to repeat significant portions of their academic work. In other words, universities should recognise the credentials awarded by colleges. Unfortunately, they are unlikely to do so unless the colleges are subject to accreditation requirements similar to those for higher education establishments. The OECD team is concerned that Latvia may not have thoroughly addressed the appropriate balance between the need for separation of colleges from universities to ensure labour-market responsiveness, and the need to ensure smooth articulation and transfer between the levels and sectors. Clarification of these points will be essential for the success of the new college sector.

Status of faculty

In 1998/99, there were 4 437 academic staff in state higher education institutions and another 747 in private institutions. The number of staff in state institutions increased by 17% from 1995/96 – a period in which the enrolments increased by 57%. In other words, the ratio of students to academic staff increased from 11:1 to 15:1. In 1997/98, the last year for which comprehensive data were available to the OECD team, the number of academic staff in state institutions identified as full-time instructional staff at "basic work" (professors, docents, lecturers and assistants) was 3064, compared to the total staff of 5184 .Comparing these data to changes in enrolments reveals a significant variation in the ratio of students to instructional staff. The average for all state institutions was 19:1, but the ratios range from 33:1 at the University of Latvia, to as few as 8:1 at the smaller institutions. These data suggest that the faculty at Latvian higher education institutions are taking on an increasing instructional burden as enrolments increase. These changes are highly uneven, however, suggesting that state policies regarding state budget and non-budget students and the allocation of resources among institutions are not matching resources with student demand and are not encouraging institutional efficiencies or optimisation.

As in the case of all countries in transition, Latvia faces a special challenge in meeting the demands for faculty in new disciplines and professions (especially in the social sciences and humanities). At the same time, large numbers of faculty remain in disciplines no longer in demand and often associated with the economy and policies of former times. Another vulnerable point is the lack of faculty in the "middle generation". Institutions face serious problems in retaining instructional staff in the face of low salaries, ageing staff, and brain-drain into the private sector. The lack of resources inhibits research capacity and the updating of equipment, and makes the higher education sector unattractive to talented young researchers. Because of low salaries, faculty members tend to teach at multiple institutions, especially at the developing private institutions. This pattern means that state universities are having increasing difficulty in ensuring students access to professors and obtaining the commitment of faculty to the basic institutional functions of academic leadership and governance. The regulations for accreditation of institutions require that academic staff "for which the higher education establishment is the primary place of employment" carry out 50% of the work.[9] Whether these requirements are sufficient to counter the tendency of institutions to utilise large numbers of part-time, "external" faculty is difficult for the OECD team to judge. Ultimately, however, fundamental improvements in the compensation and conditions of work of faculty members will be necessary to ensure the necessary quality, coherence, and numbers of faculty for Latvian higher education.

In this respect, particular attention should be given to research work and to the faculty. Basic research is perhaps the most vulnerable aspect of academic reconstruction. The former Soviet "militarist" concept of research and its placement outside universities (in Academies of Science) do not allow any simple strategy for reform. Moreover, the breakdown of the previous scientific economy and general economic reforms caused a huge decrease in the research budget. A fusion of research in universities and independent institutes is simple economic as well as a scientific necessity, while available basic research funds should be increased and focused on high-quality performers. As in the case of academic and professional studies discussed earlier, a clear distinction should be drawn between basic and applied research.

Fragmentation of higher education

Latvia's higher education system is fragmented into many small, specialised institutions, except for the University of Latvia in Riga. Efforts have been made to integrate research and teaching after the break-up of the Soviet regime, but it is questionable whether these small institutions have a large enough critical mass to perform any worthwhile scientific research. The problems relate both to the internal management of institutions as well as to the overall co-ordination, quality and cost-effectiveness of the system. The most important change occurred when Latvian universities were granted academic autonomy. This was possibly the main "shock of the transition" to higher education. Today, most critical decisions are made by academic senates. Because rectors are elected to limited terms, they often have limited executive authority. As in many other countries, this lack of executive authority presents a significant problem for institutions that must make changes that require shifts in the priorities of different faculties and may go against the interests of deeply established faculty interests. A modern higher education institution needs to deal with not only academic but also vital administrative, managerial and financial problems; but in many cases, university senates have little experience in these areas. The future development of Latvia's higher education sector is vitally dependent on the creation of more efficient managerial structures and the use of skilled personnel to support the academic leadership.

Latvian universities and other higher education institutions now operate independently, and the pressures from state bodies which characterised the former times are now no longer seen. However, a democratic and liberal society is not just the "reverse side" of a totalitarian one, and it cannot be achieved by merely negating what went before. Many of the real problems that higher education institutions encounter today that are consequences of the former period, but need to be dealt with in a new way. Therefore, institution building is a necessary part of social recovery, in higher education as much as in other social spheres. Latvian higher education institutions are clearly still under reconstruction. The traditional ones try to adapt to new circumstances; the new ones strive to establish roots as soon as possible. Among traditional institutions, the University of Latvia retains a special status, justified and protected by its reputation as the oldest national academic institution. Other traditional institutions are more vulnerable. The former system stimulated the development of narrowly specialised higher education institutions; furthermore, higher education institutions and research institutes (Academies of Sciences) were separated. There are attempts today to transform specialised institutions into more comprehensive universities by developing new disciplines. There are also many new institutions trying to find their place and establish themselves in disciplines that are in high demand.

Overall, the OECD team observed few mechanisms and incentives for institutional co-operation or synergy. The state policies for financing institutions provide few incentives for institutions to collaborate to improve the quality of education for students, strengthen research opportunities for faculty, or achieve efficiencies. Formal mechanisms such as the Council of Rectors and the Council on Higher Education are evidently unable to address inter-institutional issues that may run counter to the perceived interests of one or more of the members. The creation of an autonomous, open "space" for independent academic decisions is an important step forward; but uncoordinated policy decisions taken at the level of each individual institution could cause serious problems for the system as a whole. The need for a clear national strategy for Latvian higher education is becoming more urgent as the sector develops.

By their very nature, higher education institutions need much more stability than economic enterprises do. Therefore, they have more to gain from co-operation than from competition, and they could benefit from sensible degree of "division of labour". Competition between two city (or regional) universities in more or less the same disciplines is questionable in Latvia's present circumstances. Given the expected drop in student numbers in a few years' time, competition for these students is likely to increase; driven to extremes, this could jeopardise higher education's true mission which should be oriented toward maintaining high standards of quality, and development in the regions.

Concentration of higher education institutions in the capital is questionable not only for academic reasons; improving regional provision will help develop and stabilise regional economies and social infrastructure as well as extend opportunities for education and research to a wider pool of academic talent.

Link with national priorities

The OECD team is concerned that the mechanisms and policies are not in place in Latvia to ensure that higher education institutions contribute to major national priorities. The universities and pedagogical academies, for example, play central roles in preparing teachers as well as direct and indirect roles in-service education and professional development of existing teachers. The OECD team observed several excellent examples of university-based initiations to reform the education and professional development of teachers and to support systemic reform in general education. Yet these initiatives tended to be externally supported "pilot" projects taking place without the support of the core faculty and leadership of the universities in which they are located. Despite the high priority for reform of vocational and professional education, the OECD team observed no higher education-based initiative to train a new generation of teachers for this field. The development of new colleges will require teachers who have not only strong academic skills but also the knowledge and skill to develop high quality professional programmes. Neither the traditional career paths of university professors nor the preparation of teachers for general secondary education are appropriate for the faculty of these new institutions. In other words, systemic education reform in Latvia will require engagement of all education sectors, including higher education.

Higher education institutions should also be at the forefront of initiatives to make lifelong learning at reality in Latvia. The primary focus of most Latvian institutions, however, tends to be on youth who have recently completed secondary education. Enrolments in part-time study are increasing, but the OECD team gained the impression that part-time and correspondence study programmes have not changed significantly from the methods of previous times. These programmes are still largely peripheral to core institutional missions and the institutions often use them to generate additional revenue from fees. A commitment to lifelong learning will require fundamental restructuring of study programmes, pedagogy, and modes of programme delivery. It will also require changes in policies for institutional financing as well as tax and other policies to encourage enterprises to support and make time available for workers to continue their education and training. While Latvian leaders are clearly aware of the need for these changes, there do not appear to be means to ensure that the highly decentralised network of higher education institutions responds to these developing national priorities.

155

Nation-wide policy leadership and co-ordination

The fragmentation of Latvian higher education is mirrored at the level of state agencies. Responsibility for higher education is shared among different ministries (besides education, mainly agriculture, culture, defence, and internal affairs). As mentioned earlier, the Ministry of Education and Science and Council on Higher Education are responsible for organising accreditation of institutions and study programmes. The financing of certain disciplines, however, is traditionally the concern of the "sphere" ministry. As in the case of "budget students", the financing of higher education institutions according to their "sphere" differs considerably. Despite the difficulty of reforming traditional structures and relationships, it is essential that Latvia develop means to establish higher education priorities, and to ensure a coherent and consistent system of financing of higher education across all ministries.

State agencies can help to overcome fragmentation in higher education, but only if deliberate measures of (public) financing (and taxation) are taken. However, any such measures require full insight into the processes involved, the collection and analysis of data, and the creation of strategies. The MoES has limited capacity to provide this analysis and support for policy development. The Council on Higher Education has a responsibility to play this role, but the Council is purposely established as an entity quasi-independent from the MoES. As emphasised earlier, many of the critical education policy issues facing Latvia (access and equity, reform of vocational education, teacher training and retraining, and regional economic development) cut across units within the MoES as well as several ministries. Strengthening the policy leadership role across all agencies, perhaps with the support of the Council on Higher Education and other governmental and non-governmental organisations, should be a major priority of the Government.

The Council of Higher Education in March 1998 prepared The National Concept of the Development of Higher Education and the Institutions of Higher Education of the Republic of Latvia and submitted it to the Ministry of Education and Science and to the Cabinet of Ministers. The document intends to create main national strategies in higher education; the review team regards it as the most important strategic document so far, and hopes that its recommendations are receiving serious consideration. The document takes as its starting point the rapid growth of higher education over the past few years, but points out that future development should be based on more clear and deliberate strategies. Without such strategies, national development could be at risk. Uncertainty threatens healthy economic growth, and could hinder the integration of Latvia into the European Union. A clear strategy is also needed also to stop brain-drain, to raise a confidence in the educational system and ensure its adaptation to the labour market, and to reduce social tension and instability.

As the most urgent tasks, the National Concept proposes:

- an increase in the number of students (from 19% to 25% of each age cohort in state-funded institutions by 2005,

- administrative and academic reform of study programmes,

- differentiation of the types of institutions and an accelerated development of professional (non-university) higher education,

- accelerated and purposeful formation of young generation of teaching staff.

The document also calls for a modernisation of higher education, emphasising problem-solving in teaching and in student learning. Higher education is to be oriented on the prospective labour market. A considerable improvement of professional studies is proposed: they are to be divided into three categories (practically oriented short-term studies, medium-length studies, and studies of higher professional education), and connected with practical work and the future work place. Integration of small institutions of higher education into larger ones, and rationalisation of study programmes are proposed. Quality performance is also stressed, and a special project to increase and renew academic staff is outlined. The Concept states that the financing of higher education institutions is to be based on student demand for places. Higher education institutions should be encouraged to attract private financial means. Special emphasis is placed on the introduction of a student loan system; loans would to be provided either from the state budget, or by the institutions with state guarantees. The document elaborates both versions, sets forth the underlying principles, and analyses their positive and negative traits.[10]

The National Concept is a document of a real weight in Latvia's present circumstances. However, it is first strategic document after several years of "spontaneous", unplanned growth, and it should be the object of continuous reconsideration. As a relatively new entity, the Council of Higher Education is increasingly contributing to national strategic planning, and its work must now be fostered and harmonised with the responsibilities of the MoES as well as those of other state agencies. In due course, the Council – with their support – could evolve into to a national centre for higher education development. Given

157

the appropriate authority, it could have an important impact on the plans and decisions of higher education institutions as well as of state agencies. Help could also be given to new institutions in order to strengthen them and to encourage their collaboration or integration with other institutions.

Continuous work and co-operation by the MoES, and with support of the Council of Rectors, the Council can overcome the present fragmentation of higher education. Such a co-operation would form the basis for a more delibe-rate approach to growth, and would improve recognition of higher education as a national priority and a decisive force for national development.

Recommendations

The OECD concurs with many of the recommendations contained in the National Concept and urges that action be taken to implement them. The follo-wing recommendations reflect the specific observations and findings in the course of the review.

1. Develop the capacity at the level of the MoES for nation-wide policy lea-dership and co-ordination of tertiary education, including the developing non-university "college" sector.

 • Increase the authority of the MoES, with the advice of the Council on Higher Education, to co-ordinate higher education across all ministries. To the extent feasible, transfer institutions from other ministries to the MoES to promote a single, co-ordinated higher education system for Latvia.

 • Increase the co-ordination between the Council on Higher Education vocational education through co-ordination of policies and procedures on quality assurance, and developing common data collection and infor-mation systems.

 • Increase the representation on the Council on Higher Education of social partners and others not directly associated with institutions. This increased "public" representation would increase the ability of the Council to make recommendations in the public interest that otherwise might be blocked by narrow interests within higher education.

 • Increase attention to the connection between higher education and cros-scutting issues of education reform such as teacher education, develo-ping programmes for teachers in vocational and professional education, and strengthening the link between institutions and regional education and training networks.

2. Reform the financing of higher education, following the principles outlined in the National Concept, in order to enhance the quality, diversification, and responsiveness of the system, and to ensure access and opportunity for an increasingly diverse student population.

    - Establish a new formula for allocating state budgetary financing to institutions that takes into consideration the number of students, differences in costs among disciplines and professions, and differences in institutional missions.

    - Provide incentives for institutions to improve quality and achieve efficiencies through:

        - Implementing internal restructuring of academic programmes and services.

        - Developing alliances and collaborative agreements among institutions for joint study programmes, providing student access to study programmes and learning resources (libraries, technology) of two or more institutions (*e.g.*, institutions within Riga), and joint appointments for faculty and specialities.

        - Consolidating or merging study programmes, eliminating unnecessary duplication, and if necessary, merging or closing institutions.

    - Develop a policy framework for student financing that ensures access to qualified students without regard to socio-economic status, including:

        - A policy governing the share of costs to be borne by students through student fees.

        - Availability of student loans (credit) with rates of interest and periods for repayment that students in Latvia can afford.

        - Transparent criteria and processes for determining which students will be accepted for full or partial budgetary support.

        - Access to student loans (credit) for students enrolled in the newly developing colleges as authorised by the Law on Vocational Education and Training.

  – Provision (*e.g.*, access to loans) for students who return to higher education for additional education and training because of changes in the labour market (*e.g.*, lifelong learning).

  • Special investment funds to provide incentives for higher education institutions to collaborate with general education, vocational and professional education schools and institutions, non-governmental entities, and other organisations to support education reform.

3. Clarify the relationship of the newly developing colleges to higher education by:

  • Ensuring strong "horizontal" relationships between the colleges and the labour market.

  • Clarifying the status of colleges functioning within higher education institutions.

  • Developing policies for student transfer and programme articulation between colleges and higher education institutions and universities.

  • Co-ordinating the criteria and processes for quality assurance and accrediting higher education and colleges while ensuring that higher education criteria are not inappropriately applied to the new colleges (such as the number of faculty with the degree of doctorate).

4. Develop a more systematic, transparent relationship between the standards and examinations for completing secondary education with those for gaining entrance to higher education.

  • Develop the national examinations at completion of secondary education so that higher education institutions can use them also for student selection for admission, instead of setting separate entrance examinations.

  • Ensure that the examinations provide information for students, parents, and institutions, to encourage students to select among the diversity of tertiary education alternatives appropriate to their interests and abilities, including colleges, higher education institutions, and universities.

  Establish a university-based centre for education research and development on education. The mission of this centre would be to strengthen the capacity within Latvia to evaluate the progress of education reform, and maintain contacts with the latest developments in education research throughout the world. The centre would also undertake special research and development initiatives on assessment, curriculum development, new pedagogical approaches, issues on educational change, and other matters that are beyond the scope and capacity of entities within the MoES. While based at one university, the centre would function as an alliance drawing together the expertise of all the universities, pedagogical academies, and other institutions in Latvia.

Notes

1. Republic of Latvia, Law on Higher Education Establishments, Chapter IX.

2. Republic of Latvia, Ministry of Education and Science, Education in Latvia (Izglitiba Latvija), 1995/1996 -1998/1999, Riga 1999, p. 29.

3. Republic of Latvia, Ministry of Education and Science, Education in Latvia (Izglitiba 4. Academic information centre – ENIC/NARIC, Higher Education in Latvia, Riga, 1998/99, p. 23.

5. Republic of Latvia, Central Statistical Bureau of Latvia, Education Institutions in Latvia at the beginning of school year 1997/98, Riga, 1998, p. 100.

6. Republic of Latvia, Central Statistical Bureau of Latvia, Education Institutions in Latvia at the beginning of school year 1997/98, Riga, 1998, p. 100.

7. Republic of Latvia, Law on Higher Education Establishments, Chapter 10, section 78.

8. Republic of Latvia, Cabinet of Ministers, Accreditation Regulations for Higher Education Establishments, November 28, 1995, Regulations No. 370.

9. Republic of Latvia, Cabinet of Ministers, Accreditation Regulations for Higher Education Establishments, November 28, 1995, Regulations No. 370, section 11.13.4.

10. Republic of Latvia, Council on Higher Education, The National Concept of the Development of Higher Education and the Institutions of Higher Education of the Republic of Latvia, Riga, March 1998.

Chapter 7

Strategic Policy Development
for Education in Latvia

As reviewed in the previous sections of this report, Latvia has made significant progress in educational change since re-establishing independence. The OECD team is concerned, however, that continued progress will depend on Latvia's capacity to develop a more strategic, coherent, and systemic approach to education reform.

Stages of reform

Countries emerging from the centrally controlled, command economies of the Soviet past tend to move through several stages of development. The first is shaped by the initial euphoria with new-found freedom as the controls of the past collapse. The stage is characterised by an intense interest in reaffirming traditions and structures that preceded external domination, a proliferation of new initiatives, and decentralisation. This early stage often involves a high degree of participation of external agents each advancing a particular view of needed change.

The second stage often is a reaction to the initial proliferation and decentralisation. Efforts are made to regain national leadership and to establish standards for highly decentralised functions. The challenge is to achieve a degree of rationality and co-ordination among multiple initiatives. Yet, much like many of the early initiatives, the new frameworks tend to be externally conceived and sector-specific. Progress is measured more in terms of how well top-down initiatives are implemented than on how the education system itself (*e.g.* students, teachers, schools, and institutions) are changing to meet new challenges. The reforms lack strong connections with the country's traditions and culture and often do not reflect a genuine sense of ownership by the nation's political leadership. Because they tend to be sector-specific, they lack overall coherence.

The next stage involves efforts achieve a closer match between the early externally conceived initiatives and the country's culture, traditions and unique circumstances. The nation begins to develop its own sense of identity and traditions and refashions the earlier laws to reflect the country's own priorities, traditions and values, drawing as appropriate from the experience of others. Progress is measured in terms not only of how new reforms are implemented, but also of how change affects the long-term future of the nation's population, economy, and quality of life.

The OECD team senses that Latvia is at a critical point of transition from the second to third stages of development. The challenge now is to develop a sense of Latvian ownership, and to achieve coherence and alignment of policies with the realities of the Latvia population, economy, and culture. The focus must shift from implementing separate initiatives to shaping a public agenda for the future of Latvia. The priority should be on fostering the conditions and cultures across the diversity of Latvia that enable individuals, communities and institutions to learn and develop in the new political and economic environment. External imperatives such as the requirements for EU accession can give a sense of urgency to this development, but the concepts that give coherence must be more deeply embedded in Latvian policy and culture.

Challenges

The core challenges facing the Latvian education system discussed in the previous chapters of this review are well known to the leaders. These are articulated clearly in the documents made available to the OECD team, in conversations with the Minister and with the Parliamentary Education Commission. The challenges can be summarised as follows:

Access and equity

The challenge of access and equity is most seriously reflected in the geographic disparities (urban/rural, large and medium-sized cities and small *pagasts*) in education services, and in the remaining disparities in the capacity to speak, write, comprehend, and learn in Latvian. Yet as reflected in earlier chapters, special problems remain for children with special needs, those living in poverty and with dysfunctional families. Access remains a significant problem for more subtle reasons, such as curricula and pedagogy that do not prepare youth and adults for the labour market, for participation in civil society, and for life-long learning. Financial barriers remain insurmountable for large segments of the population, due to low wages, the costs of transportation and adequate housing, and increasing fees for higher/post-secondary education.

Quality

The challenge of quality pervades every dimension of Latvia's education system. Results of international assessments raise questions about the quality of student learning – except perhaps for those at the highest levels of achievement and those who have opportunities for access because of geographic, social and economic circumstances. Despite impressive progress in developing new standards, curricula, and assessments/examinations, a serious gap remains between educational concepts and strategies and the realities of schools and classrooms.

Perhaps the most critical quality problem is the lack of a coherent, systemic strategy to renew the human resources of Latvia's education system. The OECD team was reminded repeatedly in the course of visits to schools and universities of the dedication of Latvia's teachers, from pre-school to university. In many respects, the system has been sustained through difficult times because of these dedicated educators. Yet education reform cannot succeed when its cadre of teachers are ill-prepared for change, seriously underpaid, inefficiently utilised, inadequately trained, and inadequately supported in terms of in-service training, access to teaching materials, and basic conditions for teaching, learning, and research.

Quality is also affected by shortages in essential resources, such as textbooks that reflect new standards and curricula, teachers qualified in special fields (especially related to language and special needs), the basic infrastructure for learning (classrooms, study areas, libraries and access to information technology), and support structures for change (*e.g.* in-service training for teachers).

Efficiency

In the face of severe economic constraints, inefficiencies at every level of Latvia's education system drain resources away from efforts to address the challenges of access, equity, and quality. Among the most striking problems is the continuing, severe disparity in the capacities – both economic and political – of many *pagast*s and cities to fulfil their education responsibilities along with other social and governmental obligations. Other inefficiencies stem from widely dispersed small schools, and low teacher/pupil, faculty/student ratios that would be unsustainable in even the strongest of the world's economies. Ill-constructed and poorly insulated school facilities result in wastefully high utility costs.

Despite impressive intentions of reform in the vocational education and training system, Latvia continues to maintain a network of vocational education establishments that are still linked to the traditions, structures, and economy of the past. The system remains seriously out of touch with the changing demands of the labour market. Inadequate policies and delivery mechanisms are in place for upgrading and retraining Latvia's adult workforce. Regions have inadequate powers to ensure co-ordination and alignment of education and training resources (e.g. schools, training programmes, and labour market services) with strategies for regional economic and human resource renewal.

The early granting of autonomy to Latvia's higher education institutions shortly after re-establishment of independence has clearly contributed to significant improvements. Yet, Latvia has only limited means to ensure that its higher education institutions individually and as a system – respond to pressing national issues such as renewal of the nation's teachers in line with reforms. The legacy of the past, coupled with decentralisation and autonomy, has resulted in a highly fragmented system with few incentives and policy mechanisms to promote co-ordination, collaboration, and more efficient resource utilisation. Latvia faces a major challenge to develop a more co-ordinated, coherent, and publicly accountable higher education system while preserving the essential dimensions of academic freedom and institutional autonomy.

And finally, the institutions and sectors of Latvia's education system remain isolated from each other. Education policy is co-ordinated only in an indirect way with other social policy and services that directly affect the education of children, youth, and adults. The nation's problems concerning the health of children and families, the health and status of women, and strategies to increase the literacy and labour market skills of the adult population are inextricably linked to education, but the contacts between social and educational policy are few and the links are weak.

Policy barriers

The OECD team recognises that the Prime Minister and the Cabinet of Ministers place high priority on education reform, as exhibited in the recent statement of work. Leadership at the highest levels of the Government will be required to develop the legal and organisational frameworks to move education reform forward. The following is a summary of major barriers:

The need for public administration and civil service reform

The Government of Latvia has identified public administration and civil service reform as one of its priorities.[1] Education reform in the Republic of Latvia depends fundamentally on progress in addressing problems that cut across all dimensions of Latvian policy – far beyond education. These are important issues in the preparation for Latvia's accession to the EU – including, for example, the development of a viable sub-national regional structure. The large number of small pagasts; the limited roles for regional governmental entities; the qualification and compensation of civil servants at all levels of the system: all these have direct implications for education. Because of the central role of *pagasts* in the governance of compulsory education, disparities among *pagasts* in their capacity to maintain schools have a profound impact on the quality of educational provision. Recent reforms in the financing of compulsory education have addressed this issue to some extent. Nevertheless, the incentives for *pagasts* to provide more efficient, higher quality educational services remain limited.

As discussed in the chapter on Vocational Education and Training, a promising demonstration project for regional training centres is being implemented. Developing stronger ties between vocational/professional secondary and general secondary education is an important element of sector reform; unfortunately, Latvia's highly decentralised governance structure – and the lack of any effective regional co-ordination for general secondary – will make it difficult to establish such stronger ties.

The need for a more "systemic" approach to education reform

"Systemic" reform is a strategy that deliberately aligns the various policies that are necessary to bring about long-term improvement at the level of the classroom and, ultimately, of each student or learner. Systemic reform requires both "top-down" leadership in terms of standards and accountability and "bottom-up" change in terms of support for improvements at the level of the school, institution, *pagast* or rajon. "Bottom-up" reform takes place within the framework of national policy, but reflects far deeper professional understanding and adaptation led by individual teachers, schools, professors, universities. For vocational education and training, "bottom-up" change must involve employers, regional economic development, and other horizontal relationships.

Systemic reform requires continuous interaction at all levels, and careful alignment of policies of financing, governance, and accountability (monitoring and evaluation) with education reform goals and objectives. Systemic reform – especially reform that deliberately creates a school-level environment for individual initiative, interpretation, and creativity – contrasts sharply with the policies and culture of the past.

In Latvia, education reform appears to be a loose array of concepts, strategies, initiatives, and demonstration projects but not a coherent strategy to effect systemic change. While progress has been made regarding new standards, curricula, models, and other elements of change, the support systems for implementing these elements are highly fragmented. Critical support systems include new textbooks and instructional materials, and networks for professional development of teachers, school directors, regional school boards, inspectors, and MoES personnel. Fundamental changes are needed in the professional preparation of teachers – changes that can only be made with the full commitment and leadership of the universities. All these changes require new policies of finance and governance. In brief, new national laws will lead only to frustration and, even worse, to "compliant" implementation by schools and institutions, reflecting the culture and expectations of the previous system, unless the support systems are in place for systemic change.

Limited capacity for national leadership for education reform

The mission of the MoES combines several different roles. The MoES provides policy leadership in terms of formulating and implementing policy for the Cabinet of Ministers and Parliament (*Saeima*). It has direct operational responsibility for certain institutions (*e.g.* vocational schools under the MoES authority), and co-ordinating or oversight responsibility for vocational and professional education (especially general education) institutions under the authority of other ministries. Perhaps most importantly, the MoES prepares and adopts legislative acts for the regulation schools and institutions that are the direct responsibility of other entities – primarily *pagasts* and cities.

In OECD countries, the role of ministries is changing from the traditional emphasis on regulation, monitoring, and operations, to a more strategic leadership role with greater emphasis on technical assistance and support for systemic reform. With the world-wide emphasis on decentralisation of school and university governance, ministries can no longer rely on the same kinds of quality assurance processes that could be used in a more centralised system. New quality assurance policies – placing more emphasis on monitoring outcomes and performance rather than inputs and resources – are required to ensure that the decentralised system is accountable to public priorities. These changes in ministries' roles require personnel with significantly different skills and "mentalities" from those of the past. Critical attributes include more emphasis on strategic thinking, openness to extensive participation of communication with schools, teachers, and social partners, a commitment to transparency, and a strong disposition toward serving and supporting "bottom-up" change.

The OECD team is concerned that the MoES in Latvia is seriously challenged in its capacity to accomplish its current legal mandate. The MoES is not well positioned to make the transition to the more strategic leadership role that is required to move education reform in Latvia forward. While Latvia has developed impressive concepts and strategies and enacted progressive changes in its legal framework, its capacity to implement these changes is weak. The MoES has been hampered by frequent changes in the Minister of Education and Science, and a staff that is clearly dedicated but poorly compensated and supported for its responsibilities. The seriously understaffed MoES appears caught between the obligations to carry out operational and regulatory tasks reflecting out-dated laws and policies, on the one hand, and the expectation that it take on entirely new roles, on the other. Limited co-ordinating capacity across organisational units results in a high degree of fragmentation and undermines the MoES capacity to support systemic reform. The reorganisation of the MoES in 1999 to place both general and vocational education under the same Deputy State Secretary, and to establish a position of Deputy State Secretary on Educational Strategy and International Co-operation, appear to be important steps to strengthen the MoES' capacity for strategic direction and co-ordination.

Despite the responsibility of the MoES as the principal education agency for the Republic, the Ministry has limited authority and ability to carry out that role with respect to other ministries and especially related to higher education. Latvia continues to divide responsibility for vocational education among several sectoral ministries, a practice that reflects the structure of the Soviet command economy. If Latvia retains such divided operational responsibility for vocational and professional education, it will nonetheless be increasingly important to develop co-ordinated strategies for vocational education and training at both the national and regional levels and cutting across all ministries. This co-ordinating role is important for all education levels and sectors. It was uncertain at the time of the OECD review whether the MoES could lead such a strategy – without broader legal authority and stronger support of the Government.

The MoES's authority related to higher education is severely limited by the legal protections of institutional autonomy and the fact that the Council on Higher Education operates independent of the direct authority of the Minister of Education and Science. As emphasised in the chapter of this review on higher education, the OECD team respects the arguments favouring a degree of autonomy of this sector from direct governmental intrusion. Nevertheless, it is critical that Latvia's higher education system be linked more effectively with strategies for reform of general education and vocational education and training. Fundamental change in the universities' roles in teacher education and education research are core elements of the nation's capacity for change. The universities' entrance requirements directly affect the standards and expectations for the secondary education system. Yet the MoES has little policy levera-

ge to ensure that the nation's higher education system responds to these imperatives.

Other issues that are directly related to education and education reform,
such as the health and welfare of children and families, are the not the direct
responsibility of the MoES. It appears that co-ordination across ministries on
these issues occurs primarily through the Cabinet of Ministers and various parliamentary commissions.

External assistance, primarily through EC-Phare, has been invaluable in
developing more strategic thinking and developing the infra-structure for change: new policies, strengthened research and information services, networks with
schools, institutions and social partners, and a promising network of pilot and
demonstration projects. The problem is that these initiatives have occurred largely outside the MoES. The most prominent initiatives appear to have focused
largely on vocational education and training, with less impact on the largest
MoES responsibility – that for general education. At the time of the OECD
review, it was uncertain whether the Republic of Latvia could assume financial
responsibility for these initiatives after external support ceases.

As mentioned several times in this review, Latvia has made impressive progress in developing the basic legal framework for education reform. The Latvian
Concept of Education adopted in 1995 provided a foundation for subsequent
development of laws. Yet, in spite of the 1995 Concept, the OECD team gained
an impression that Latvia has developed multiple legal frameworks without a
widely recognised and accepted overarching concept of reform that gives coherence to all education in Latvia. There is no strategy that links education to other
major national priorities such as the health and welfare of families and children,
economic and workforce development, and development of civil society. The Law
on Education and the other framework laws are important in defining the legal
status, governance, and financing of various schools, institutions, and entities.
These laws, however, cannot alone constitute a compelling public agenda for the
future of education in Latvia.

Latvia also faces a major challenge in sustaining attention to education
reform. From the re-establishment of independence, Latvia has pursued consistent themes in education reform. Nevertheless, frequent changes in government,
including Ministers of Education and Science, have seriously affected the capacity of the Government to lead a sustained agenda of change and improvement.
At the time of the OECD review, the Minister was committed to leading a change in the role of the MoES, yet his ability to do so depended on support from the
Cabinet of Ministers. As the OECD understands the governmental structure of

the Republic of Latvia, shaping and leading a nation-wide strategy for education is ultimately the responsibility of the Government and the Cabinet of Ministers. While the latest Statement of Work adopted in July 1999 demonstrates a commitment to education reform, the agenda remains one of specific work plans for different sector ministries. No attention is given to the crosscutting, co-ordinated strategy that is essential for long-term sustained improvement of the nation's education system. The statement does not reflect recognition at the highest levels of government that improving the quality of education is fundamental to the solution of virtually every priority facing Latvia. Education is central to Latvia's efforts to achieve social integration, develop a civil society, develop a competitive market economy, and narrow the disparities in wealth and opportunities of all the population.

Recommendations

1.   Establish at the level of the President of the Republic a mechanism (a task force or commission) to shape and gain consensus around, and sustain attention to, a general concept and strategy for long-term improvement of education in Latvia. This general concept and strategy should encompass all sectors and dimensions of education (including life-long learning) as encompassed in the 1998 Law on Education. It should make clear the links between education and the major social and economic challenges facing Latvia in the next decade and beyond. It should be shaped with extensive engagement of the major stakeholders across Latvia – students, parents, teachers and school directors, universities, trade unions, enterprises, municipal government (*pagasts*), non-governmental organisations, and political leaders. The development process should make extensive use of public forums and use of the media in every region of Latvia. It should include specific, measurable benchmarks for improvement of education in Latvia over a five to ten-year period utilising the OECD indicators for the purpose of international comparisons. This recommendation emphasises the level of the President of the Republic, because of the need for sustained attention to the general concept and strategy even as governments change. The intent would not be to supplant existing law, but to promote coherence and co-ordination among multiple initiatives across Latvia – public and non-public, formal and informal, local as well as national, externally or locally initiated – that contribute to the long-term goals.

2.   Reach agreement and implement public administration and civil service reforms that are essential for effective governance, co-ordination, and oversight of education at all levels – *pagasts*, *rajons*, cities, and national

171

government. These reforms should include regional mechanisms to ensure co-ordination of all available education and training resources (*e.g.* vocational education and training, general education, and adult education) to meet the needs of each region within Latvia.

3. Redefine the role and responsibilities of the Ministry of Education and Science to emphasise strategic leadership, co-ordination of education policy across all ministries, and support for systemic education reform. In the course of the OECD review, the MoES clearly indicated an intention to move in these directions, and, as indicated earlier, the reorganisation of the MoES in 1999 made important improvements. Nevertheless, in the view of the OECD team, more decisive actions, backed by the Cabinet of Ministers, are necessary to move education reform from strategies and concepts to implementation and school-level change. Because of the likely continuing limitations in the numbers of qualified staff and funding available for ministry functions, it is especially important that limited resources be focused on priority tasks. The following are suggested priorities:

  • Develop a stronger strategic planning and co-ordinating unit at the level of the Minister with responsibility to develop strategies that cut across all ministries and all divisions and departments within the MoES. For example, strategies related to standards, examinations and curricula for general education have direct implications for vocational education. In addition, the MoES should be the co-ordinating unit across all the government regarding education policy that affects the health and welfare of children and families.

  • Strengthen the school and institution-level leadership of schools and institutions for which the MoES has direct responsibility (*e.g.*, vocational schools), and change the MoES role from direct operation to co-ordination, quality assurance, and technical assistance.

  • Strengthen the capabilities of the MoES for policy analysis, research, and evaluation of policy implementation. At the time of the OECD review, these capabilities were limited and strongly dependent upon external assistance.

  • Strengthen the capabilities of the MoES to support systemic education reform. Perhaps the most important change would be for the MoES to co-ordinate implementation of separate initiatives with a clear sense of how these initiatives affect school-level change. For example, this would mean giving top priority to co-ordinating new national examinations, curricular requirements, development of textbooks and teaching materials, professional development of teachers, reform of teacher education, and other essential elements of systemic reform throughout the system.

- Strengthen the support network for change by decentralising the support network to regional school boards, and greatly strengthening the co-ordination of projects, pilots, and initiatives of external foreign partners and non-governmental organisations (NGOs). A number of externally funded, foreign assistance projects (EC/Phare, ETF, Soros Foundation, British Council, Nordic Council of Ministers, German and Danish donor agencies, the World Bank, and the UNDP, to mention only the most prominent) are providing invaluable support for education reform in Latvia. Much of this support is for pilot and demonstration projects, and will eventually cease. Because the MoES resources are limited, it is essential that the MoES play a stronger role in co-ordinating multiple external projects to support long-term, sustainable, systemic reform. Greater use of NGOs to facilitate this co-ordination and communication may be an effective strategy if and when it would be inappropriate or impossible for the MoES to play these roles directly.

- Strengthen the authority and capacity of the MoES to engage Latvia's higher education institutions in addressing the major educational, social, and economic challenges facing the nation. While academic freedom and a degree of autonomy are essential for strong universities, these institutions have a fundamental public responsibility to contribute to major national priorities, and should be publicly accountable for this responsibility. A portion of the public funding of these institutions should be contingent upon their support for these priorities. Reform of teacher education, developing initiatives for education of teachers for vocational and professional education, a commitment to stronger professional development of teachers, and commitments to education research, are examples of essential contributions of Latvia's universities to education reform.

4. Recognize the important role of the *Saeima* (including the Education, Culture and Science Commission in:

- Evaluating and approving education development programmes developed by the Cabinet of Ministers, and

- In accordance with the regulations "*Saeimas kartibas rullis*", providing parliamentary supervision of the activities of the Ministry of Education and Science.

173

5.   Align financing policy with a strategy for long-term improvement of education in Latvia. Priorities in this alignment should be to:

- Implement reforms enacted in the past few years moving toward norm-based, per-student funding of general education and vocational and professional education.

- Implement reforms designed to ensure access and opportunity at the tertiary education level, including policies (some already resolved in Latvia) related to state funding of student places, student fees, and student loan policies.

- Provide incentives for social partners to participate in education reform (*e.g.*, providing work-place experiences for students, contributing equipment and other material for training, and participating in new systems for identifying labour market needs and professional qualification schemes).

- Provide funding, through deliberate action of the Government and *Saeima*, to support the essential elements of systemic reform in addition to the funding provided to schools and teachers for wages and social benefits for school personnel. Examples include funding for adequate capacity at the MoES for strategic leadership, policy analysis, and research. Funding should also be targeted for incentives to universities to reform teacher education and contribute to professional development of education personnel, development of instructional materials, and other support systems for schools and institutions.

Education in Latvia, as this review demonstrates, faces a number of complex problems and challenges. Yet Latvia's schools are lively and optimistic places, where innovations mix with old-fashioned values to produce a learning environment that, given sustained and coherent support, could stand comparison with the best to be found in Europe. This, in a nutshell, was the main impression the OECD team received; and while it may sound facile and is undoubtedly superficial, it draws a useful distinction between the status of educational reform and day-to-day school life. This review is about that distinction, and about policy efforts that could be made to support the work of schools and universities, and the future lives of Latvia's children and youth.

Notes

1.   Republic of Latvia, Declaration of the Work of the Cabinet of Ministers, 15 July 2000.

Selected Bibliography

AINSCOW, Mel, and MEMMENASHA Haile-Giorgis. "The Education of Children with Special Needs: Barriers and Opportunities in Central and Eastern Europe". Innocenti Occasional Papers, Economic and Social Policy Series, no. 67. Florence: UNICEF International Child Development Centre,1998.

DREIFELDS, Juris. Latvia in Transition. Cambridge: Cambridge University Press, 1996.

DREIMANE, Anna "Special Education in Latvia". Riga: General Education Department, Ministry of Education and Science, 1998. Mimeo.

European Commission, Agenda 2000: Commission Opinion on Latvia's Application for Membership of the European Union, June 1997.

Academic Information Centre – Latvian National Observatory. Vocational education in Latvia. Riga: 1999.

European Training Foundation National Observatory. Latvia: National Report on the VET System. Recent Changes, Challenges and Reform Needs. Riga, 1998: ETF-Observatory Unit.

Latvian National Observatory country report. Report on vocational education and training system – Latvia 1999, European Training Foundation, 2000.

Academic Information Centre – Latvia National Observatory, Analysis of the Response of the VET System to the New Economic Objectives in Latvia. Riga: 1998.

Henley, Maria and Alexandrova, Anastassia (1999). "Children in Institutionalised Public Care in Russia." Washington: The World Bank. Unpublished report.

Higher School for Social Work and Social Pedagogy 'Attistiba' and the Centre for Criminological Research. Project "Child in the Street". Riga: 1997.

Republic of Latvia. General Education Law (Draft). Unpublished draft under discussion in the *Saeima*. Riga: February 1999.

– Law on Education. Riga: *Saeima*, 1991.

– Human Rights for Human Development." "Latvia's Contribution to the Report from the Commission on Latvia's Progress Toward Accession (National Progress Report), Riga, June 1999.

– National Report on the Implementation of the Convention on the Rights of the Child: Latvia. Joint report compiled by the Ministries of Health, Justice, Education and Science, Interior, Foreign Affairs, Culture, Environment Protection and Regional Development, Economy; the State Statistics Committee; the State Coroner's Medical centre, National AIDS Centre; Save the Children, Latvian Children's Fund etc. Riga: 1997.

– "Latvia's Contribution to the Report from the Commission on Latvia's Progress Toward Accession" (National Progress Report). Riga: June 1999.

– Cabinet of Ministers. "Declaration of the Proposed Activities by the Cabinet of Ministers". Riga: 6 January 1999.

– Cabinet of Ministers. "Declaration on the Work of the Cabinet of Ministers" Riga: July 1999.

– Central Statistical Bureau. Education Institutions in Latvia at the Beginning of School Year 1997/98. Riga: 1998.

– Central Statistical Bureau. Who Seeks Job in Latvia?: Elements of Analysis of the Unemployment Situation in Latvia. Data on 1997. Riga: 1998.

– Ministry of Economy. Economic Development of Latvia. Riga: December 1998,

– Ministry of Education and Science. Education in Latvia, 1995/96 to 1998/99. Riga: MoES, 1999.

– Ministry of Education and Science. Centre for Curriculum Development and Examinations (ISEC). National Standards of Compulsory Education Riga: MoES, 1998.

– Ministry of Education and Science. Cabinet of Ministers Regulation No. 194, "Regulations for Registration of School-Age Children"; and MoES Instruction "On the Compulsory Registration of School-Age Children". Riga: 1996.

– Ministry of Foreign Affairs. "History, Language, Identity and Culture of Latvia," www.mfa.gov.lv.

– Ministry of Foreign Affairs. Human Rights and Social Integration in the Republic of Latvia: A General Survey. National Report of Latvia Ministry of Foreign Affairs and Nationalisation Board for the United Nations Development Programme Regional Meeting in Yalta 22-4 September 1998

– Ministry of Local Affairs. Local Government Budget 1997, Riga, 1997.

– State Employment Service. "Registered Unemployment and Unemployment Rates by Locality." Riga: SES, December 1998.

– Ministry of Welfare. Social Report 1998. Riga: 1998.

– School Curriculum and Assessment Authority (SCAA) and the University of Durham. The Value-Added National Project: Final Report. Feasibility Studies for a National System of Value-Added Indicators. London: 1997.

– Seile, Marite. "The Situation in Latvian Teacher In-Service Education: Needs Assessment". Riga: Soros Foundation Latvia, 1997. Mimeo.

– UNICEF. Children at Risk in Central and Eastern Europe: Perils and Promises. Regional Monitoring Report No. 4, UNICEF International Child Development Centre. Florence: ICDC, 1997.

– Education for All? .Regional Monitoring Report No. 5, UNICEF International Child Development Centre. Florence: ICDC, 1997.

– United Nations Development Programme. "National Integration and Social Cohesion," Latvia: Human Development Report. Riga: UNDP, 1997.

– Latvia Human Development Report 1998. Riga: 1998.

Vári, Péter (ed.) Are We Similar in Math and Science? A Study of Grade 8 in Nine Central and Eastern European Countries. Budapest: IEA/TIMSS, 1997. C/EE countries participating included Bulgaria, Czech Republic, Hungary, Latvia,

Lithuania, Romania, Russian Federation, the Slovak Republic, and Slovenia.

The World Bank, Republic of Latvia "Education Sector Strategy Paper". Washington: August 1998.

The World Bank, ECSHD. "Project Appraisal Document (and Annexes) on a Proposed Loan to the Republic of Latvia for an Education Improvement Project". Washington: January 19, 1999.

OECD PUBLICATIONS, 2, rue André-Pascal, 75775 PARIS CEDEX 16
PRINTED IN FRANCE
(14 2001 07 1P) ISBN 92-64-18641-7 – No. 51773 2001